THE END OF THE SENTENCE

HMP Holloway was the largest women's prison in Europe, historically holding numerous infamous female criminals and eliciting intrigue and fascination from the public. *The End of the Sentence: Psychotherapy with Female Offenders* documents the rich and varied psychotherapeutic work undertaken by dedicated specialists in this intense and often difficult environment, where attempts to provide psychological security were often undermined by conflicting ideas of physical security.

Women commit crime most often in the context of poverty, addiction and transgenerational violence or trauma, familial cycles of offending and imprisonment which are often overlooked. Using personal testimony and case studies, and screened through the lens of psychoanalytic theory, the book examines the enduring therapeutic and relational endeavour to find connection, closure and to experience a "good enough" ending with prisoners when the possibility of a positive new beginning often seemed remote. It also considers how the cultural and political discourse remains hostile towards women who are incarcerated, and how this may have culminated in the closure of the only female prison in London.

Through real-life accounts, this insightful book also emphasizes the importance of professionals finding ways of supporting one another to offer women who have entered the criminal justice system a way to leave it. It will prove fascinating reading for forensic psychotherapists, forensic psychologists and criminologists, as well as anyone interested in the criminal justice system.

Pamela Windham Stewart has worked for over twenty years as a psychotherapist in a number of prisons where she has developed and facilitated therapy groups for mothers and babies who are incarcerated. Pamela lectures widely and is the founder of the Saturday Forensic Forum. She has a private practice and is a clinical supervisor.

Jessica Collier is an art psychotherapist and clinical supervisor working with women in the female prison estate. She lectures widely on forensic art psychotherapy and her published work focuses on trauma and unconscious re-enactments in forensic institutions. Jessica is co-convenor of the Forensic Arts Therapies Advisory Group and visiting lecturer at the University of Hertfordshire.

FORENSIC PSYCHOTHERAPY MONOGRAPH SERIES
Series Editor: Professor Brett Kahr
Honorary Consultant: Dr Estela V. Welldon

Other titles in the Series

Violence: A Public Health Menace and a Public Health Approach
    Edited by Sandra L. Bloom

Life within Hidden Walls: Psychotherapy in Prisons
    Edited by Jessica Williams Saunders

Forensic Psychotherapy and Psychopathology: Winnicottian Perspectives
    Edited by Brett Kahr

Dangerous Patients: A Psychodynamic Approach to Risk Assessment and Management
    Edited by Ronald Doctor and Sarah Nettleton

Anxiety at 35,000 Feet: An Introduction to Clinical Aerospace Psychology
    Robert Bor

The Mind of the Paedophile: Psychoanalytic Perspectives
    Edited by Charles W. Socarides and Loretta R. Loeb

Violent Adolescents: Understanding the Destructive Impulse
    Edited by Lynn Greenwood

Violence in Children: Understanding and Helping Those Who Harm
    Edited by Rosemary Campher

Murder: A Psychotherapeutic Investigation
    Edited by Ronald Doctor

Psychic Assaults and Frightened Clinicians: Countertransference in Forensic Settings
    Edited by John Gordon and Gabriel Kirtchuk

Forensic Aspects of Dissociative Identity Disorder
    Edited by Adah Sachs and Graeme Galton

Playing with Dynamite: A Personal Approach to the Psychoanalytic Understanding of Perversions, Violence, and Criminality
    Estela V. Welldon

The Internal World of the Juvenile Sex Offender: Through a Glass Darkly then Face to Face
    Timothy Keogh

Disabling Perversions: Forensic Psychotherapy with People with Intellectual Disabilities
    Alan Corbett

Sexual Abuse and the Sexual Offender: Common Man or Monster?
    Barry Maletzky

Psychotherapy with Male Survivors of Sexual Abuse: The Invisible Men
    Alan Corbett

Consulting to Chaos: An Approach to Patient-Centred Reflective Practice
    Edited by John Gordon, Gabriel Kirtchuk, Maggie McAlister, and David Reiss

THE END OF THE SENTENCE

Psychotherapy with Female Offenders

Edited by
*Pamela Windham Stewart and
Jessica Collier*

Routledge
Taylor & Francis Group
LONDON AND NEW YORK

First published 2019
by Routledge
2 Park Square, Milton Park, Abingdon, Oxon OX14 4RN

and by Routledge
711 Third Avenue, New York, NY 10017

Routledge is an imprint of the Taylor & Francis Group, an informa business

© 2019 editorial matter and individual chapters, Pamela Windham Stewart and Jessica Collier; other individual chapters, the contributors

The right of Pamela Windham Stewart and Jessica Collier to be identified as the authors of the editorial material, and of the authors for their individual chapters, has been asserted in accordance with sections 77 and 78 of the Copyright, Designs and Patents Act 1988.

All rights reserved. No part of this book may be reprinted or reproduced or utilised in any form or by any electronic, mechanical, or other means, now known or hereafter invented, including photocopying and recording, or in any information storage or retrieval system, without permission in writing from the publishers.

Trademark notice: Product or corporate names may be trademarks or registered trademarks, and are used only for identification and explanation without intent to infringe.

British Library Cataloguing-in-Publication Data
A catalogue record for this book is available from the British Library

Library of Congress Cataloging-in-Publication Data
A catalogue record for this book has been requested

ISBN: 978-0-367-07431-9 (hbk)
ISBN: 978-0-367-07432-6 (pbk)
ISBN: 978-0-429-02072-8 (ebk)

Typeset in Palatino
by Swales & Willis Ltd

Printed and bound in Great Britain by
TJ International Ltd, Padstow, Cornwall

CONTENTS

ACKNOWLEDGEMENTS   viii
SERIES EDITOR'S FOREWORD   ix
EDITORS AND CONTRIBUTORS   xv
FOREWORD BY ESTELA WELLDON   xix

Introduction   1
   Jessica Collier

PART I
PRISON AND THE SYMBOLIC MOTHER

CHAPTER ONE
The violence of austerity   9
   Maureen Mansfield

CHAPTER TWO
Twenty years in prison: reflections on the birth of the Born Inside
project and psychotherapy in HMP Holloway   23
   Pamela Windham Stewart

CHAPTER THREE
Who's holding the baby? Containment, dramatherapy and the
pregnant therapist   41
   Lorna Downing and Lorraine Grout

PART II
WORKING WITH INSTITUTIONAL DYNAMICS

CHAPTER FOUR
Encountering HMP Holloway: a conversation 59
Paola Franciosi and Karen Rowe

CHAPTER FIVE
Challenges: working at the boundary of confinement and freedom 72
Kimberley Wilson

CHAPTER SIX
Parallel endings: a personal reflection on the closure of HMP Holloway 85
Chrissy Reeves

PART III
LIVING IN PRISON

CHAPTER SEVEN
Living and dying: a journey through the life cycle of the Onyx art therapy group for women from overseas 101
Siobhan Lennon and Zoe Atkinson

CHAPTER EIGHT
"I will never get out of here": therapeutic work with an Imprisonment for Public Protection prisoner caught up in the criminal justice system 123
Sabina Amiga

CHAPTER NINE
"I could do it on my eyelashes": holding the unthinkable for the unthinking patient 137
Frances Maclennan and Catherine McCoy

PART IV
PRISON AND SOCIETY

CHAPTER TEN
Holloway and after: from loss to creativity　153
　Sophie Benedict

CHAPTER ELEVEN
Trauma, art and the "borderspace": working with unconscious
re-enactments　164
　Jessica Collier

Afterword　183
　Jessica Collier and Pamela Windham Stewart

INDEX　185

ACKNOWLEDGEMENTS

The case material in this book has been used throughout with permission from the individuals with whom the authors worked. We are grateful to them for allowing us to share their experiences and the insights they offered.

We would like to thank Brett Kahr for his generous and enthusiastic approach and encouragement in the making of this book.

In the years before its closure our clinical work at HMP Holloway was supervised by Professor Gill McGauley. She was a deeply supportive and inspiring colleague, and we hope this book is imbued with her warmth and generosity.

SERIES EDITOR'S FOREWORD

Brett Kahr

Throughout human history, prisons have served, first and foremost, as places of punishment, in which the long-standing philosophy of *lex talionis* – the law of talion – would be enacted with vengeance. Indeed, our ancestors performed cruel retributions upon prisoners, perfecting the notion of "an eye for an eye". Whether the ancient Greek *desmoterion* or the ancient Roman *carcer*, penal institutions have flourished, often treating inmates with great sadism.

During the late eighteenth century, the Englishman John Howard lobbied for prison reform, as a result of which, incarcerated men and women began to receive better food and care within their cells (e.g., Howard, 1958; Southwood, 1958; Radzinowicz, 1978). Throughout the nineteenth century, the prison reform movement made great strides, campaigning for more protective legislation. But not until the introduction of psychoanalysis in the early twentieth century would penal institutions begin to flirt with a more compassionate approach to the rehabilitation of offender-patients (Kahr, 2018).

As early as 1907, Professor Sigmund Freud lambasted the horrors of penal institutions, lamenting the "unsinnige Behandlung dieser Leute (soweit sie Demenz zeigen) in Gefängnissen" (quoted in Rank, 1907a: 101), which translates as the "nonsensical treatment of these people in prisons (in so far as they are demented)" (quoted in Rank, 1907b: 108). Freud certainly transmitted his compassionate attitude to his followers, including the Hungarian psychoanalyst, Dr Sándor Ferenczi (1922), who wrote about the vile manner in which guards would often mishandle their prisoners.

It remains unclear when, precisely, psychoanalysts first began to work in prisons but, certainly, by the 1930s, a number of German Freudian practitioners had begun to do so, notably the Berlin physician and novelist, Dr Alfred Döblin (1924). In similar vein, the early Adlerian psychotherapist, Herr Fritz Kleist (1931), occupied a pioneering role in the history of forensic psychotherapy by having offered both individual and group treatment to offenders in a prison at Celle, near Hannover, in Germany.

Across the twentieth century, prison psychotherapy spread across diverse territories, ranging from Argentina (Abraham, 1924) to Lexington, Kentucky (Chessick, 2018). Psychoanalysts worked hard not only to worm their way *into* the prison but, also, laboured intensively to get inmates *out*. Most famously, the French psychoanalyst, Princess Marie Bonaparte, petitioned both Edmund Brown, the governor of California, and John Fitzgerald Kennedy, the American president, pleading for the release of the convicted criminal, Caryl Chessman, then serving on death row in the California State Prison in San Quentin, albeit to no avail (Bertin, 1982).

British mental health professionals, as well, worked hard to introduce psychological ideas into the prison system. In 1924, the English psychiatrist Dr Maurice Hamblin Smith (1924), an early Associate Member of the British Psycho-Analytical Society, argued that inmates should receive treatment in hospitals, as many suffered from mental illnesses, rather than punishment in prisons. A sometime Medical Officer at HM Prison Winson Green in Birmingham, Smith may hold the distinction as the first Freudian-orientated Briton to practise within the penal system.

Some years later, Dr John Charsley Mackwood built upon the pioneering work of Dr Maurice Hamblin Smith by introducing psychodynamic psychotherapy as part of the rehabilitation of mentally troubled offenders at Wormwood Scrubs Prison in London. Recognising that psychoanalysis requires an immense investment of time and resources, Mackwood (1949, 1952) championed group psychotherapy for offender-patients. The English psychoanalyst Dr Arthur Hyatt Williams (1964), who succeeded Mackwood at Wormwood Scrubs, continued to develop this work during the 1960s, while, in the 1970s, the psychiatrist Dr Murray Cox (1979) did likewise at HM Pentonville, also, in London (cf. Kahr, 2000).

Her Majesty's Prison Holloway, the subject of this wonderful new book edited by Pamela Windham Stewart and Jessica Collier, occupies an important place not only in the history of British criminology and psychology but, also, within the wider context of British history more generally. Founded in London in 1852, the Holloway prison served as a house of punishment for innumerable men and women, not least many of the suffragettes, such as Christabel Pankhurst and, also, Emily Wilding Davison, who eventually committed suicide by hurling herself underneath George V's horse, Anmer, at the Epsom Derby in 1913. During the Second World War, the Fascist leader Sir Oswald Mosley lived in a cottage on the prison's grounds, along with his wife Diana, Lady Mosley. Perhaps, most notoriously of all, Holloway served as a prison for the infamous Myra Hindley, convicted for her participation in the cruel murders of many children during the 1960s.

Like most British prisons, Holloway punished its inmates with incarceration and, sometimes, capital punishment. The prison hanged at least five women during the twentieth century, including, in 1955, Ruth Ellis, the last female murderess subjected to execution in Great Britain.

It took quite some time before Her Majesty's Prison Holloway embraced more enlightened psychological approaches to the care of its mentally troubled inmates. Indeed, to the best of my knowledge, the first "Freudian" to enter the prison did so as a punishment for being an enemy alien.

In 1938, Professor Sigmund Freud, a refugee from Nazi-infested Austria, emigrated to England, where he would spend the final months of his life. He travelled to London with his wife, Frau Professor Martha Freud, his daughter, Fräulein Anna Freud, and also a physician, Dr Josefine Stross, as well as his long-standing housekeeper, the devoted Fräulein Paula Fichtl, who had worked for the family over many years.

After the outbreak of the Second World War, the British government treated many refugees with considerable suspicion, and Fräulein Fichtl had her passport confiscated as an enemy alien. In 1940, not long after the death of Sigmund Freud, an officer from Scotland Yard arrived at the Freud family home on Maresfield Gardens in Swiss Cottage, North London, and arrested Fichtl, and then drove her in a Black Maria police vehicle to Holloway prison, where she remained for a time, in a cell, prior to her deportation to the Rushen Interment Camp in Port Erin on the Isle of Man. Eventually, Freud's aristocratic colleague, the aforementioned Marie Bonaparte, had to call upon none other than Winston Churchill to arrange for Fichtl's eventual release (Berthelsen, 1987). Thus, Paula Fichtl may hold the distinction as Holloway's first psychotherapeutically informed resident.

Happily, in the decades which followed, various mental health workers began to apply psychodynamic ideas more formally to the rehabilitation of the women of Holloway, many of whom suffered from profound psychological illnesses and vulnerabilities. Sadly, in spite of this valiant, path-breaking work, Holloway prison closed in 2016, depriving numerous female inmates of a sanctuary.

This extraordinary book, *The End of the Sentence: Psychotherapy with Female Offenders*, chronicles the very pioneering efforts undertaken by many of the psychoanalytically informed members of staff who contributed to the amelioration of prison life at this formidable institution. In a series of creative, original chapters, Windham Stewart, Collier, and their many colleagues, describe in graphic detail the moving ways in which they have drawn upon psychological understanding to work therapeutically with many of these dangerous and, also, tormented, women.

Prison psychotherapy remains a relatively new development within mental health for the simple reason that we, as human beings, have committed ourselves far too enthusiastically to *punishment* rather than to *rehabilitation*. But I predict that prison psychotherapy will become, increasingly, the gold standard approach, rather than an occasional luxury.

In 2001, the Forensic Psychotherapy Monograph Series, in which this new title appears, launched with the publication of the first British book on prison psychotherapy, Jessica Williams Saunders's (2001) edited collection, *Life within Hidden Walls: Psychotherapy in Prisons*. At that time, nearly two decades ago, Saunders's book – a worthy and well-prepared study – attracted very little attention outside of forensic mental health circles, in part, because virtually no one knew that professionals *could* work psychotherapeutically with offenders. But now, in 2018, the climate has changed considerably, and I regularly encounter young psychotherapy and counselling trainees who have obtained clinical placements working in prison settings across the country.

I earnestly hope that the visionary labours of Pamela Windham Stewart, Jessica Collier, and their comrades – described so clearly and so passionately in the pages herein – will serve not only as a testimonial to their valiant work at Her Majesty's Prison Holloway but, also, will, inspire future generations of forensic mental health professionals and volunteers to help us transform our prisons from houses of punishment into clinics for care.

REFERENCES

Abraham, Karl. (1924). Letter to Sigmund Freud. 25th May. In Ernst Falzeder and Ludger M. Hermanns (Eds.), *Sigmund Freud and Karl Abraham (2009). Briefwechsel 1907–1925: Vollständige Ausgabe. Band 2: 1915–1925*, pp. 765–766. Vienna: Verlag Turia und Kant.

Berthelsen, Detlef. (1987). *Alltag bei Familie Freud: Die Erinnerungen der Paula Fichtl*. Hamburg: Hoffmann und Campe Verlag.

Bertin, Célia. (1982). *La Dernière Bonaparte*. Paris: Librairie Académique Perrin.

Chessick, Richard D. (2018). *Apologia Pro Vita Mea: An Intellectual Odyssey*. Abingdon: Routledge.

Cox, Murray. (1979). Dynamic Psychotherapy with Sex-Offenders. In Ismond Rosen (Ed.), *Sexual Deviation: Second Edition*, pp. 306–350. Oxford: Oxford University Press.

Döblin, Alfred. (1924). *Die beiden Freundinnen und ihr Giftmord*. Berlin: Verlag die Schmiede.

Ferenczi, Sándor. (1922). *Populäre Vorträge über Psychoanalyse*. Vienna: Internationaler Psychoanalytischer Verlag.

Howard, Derek L. (1958). *John Howard: Prison Reformer*. London: Christopher Johnson.

Kahr, Brett. (2000). In Memoriam: Dr Murray Cox. *Psychotherapy Review*, 2, 214–215.

Kahr, Brett. (2018). "No Intolerable Persons" or "Lewd Pregnant Women": Towards a History of Forensic Psychoanalysis. In Brett Kahr (Ed.), *New Horizons in Forensic Psychotherapy: Exploring the Work of Estela V. Welldon*, pp. 17–87. London: Karnac Books.

Kleist, Fritz. (1931). Erfahrungen eines Individualpsychologen im Strafvollzug. *Internationale Zeitschrift für Individualpsychologie*, 9, 381–388.

Mackwood, John C. (1949). The Psychological Treatment of Offenders in Prison. *British Journal of Psychology: General Section*, 40, 5–22.

Mackwood, John. (1952). Group Therapy in Prisons. *Howard Journal*, 8, 104–112.

Radzinowicz, Leon. (1978). John Howard. In John C. Freeman (Ed.), *Prisons Past and Future*, pp. 7–13. London: Heinemann/Heinemann Educational Books.

Rank, Otto. (1907a). Vortragsabend: Am 6. Februar 1907. In Herman Nunberg and Ernst Federn (Eds.). (1976). *Protokolle der Wiener Psychoanalytischen Vereinigung: Band I. 1906–1908*, pp. 97–104. Frankfurt am Main: S. Fischer/S. Fischer Verlag.

Rank, Otto. (1907b). Scientific Meeting on February 6, 1907. In Herman Nunberg and Ernst Federn (Eds.). (1962). *Minutes of the Vienna Psychoanalytic Society: Volume I: 1906–1908* (Margarethe Nunberg (Transl.)), pp. 103–110. New York: International Universities Press.

Saunders, Jessica Williams (Ed.). (2001). *Life within Hidden Walls: Psychotherapy in Prisons*. London: H. Karnac (Books).

Smith, Maurice Hamblin. (1924). The Mental Conditions Found in Certain Sexual Offenders, *The Lancet*, 29 March, 643–646.

Southwood, Martin. (1958). *John Howard: Prison Reformer. An Account of His Life and Travels*. London: Independent Press.

Williams, Arthur Hyatt. (1964). The Psychopathology and Treatment of Sexual Murderers. In Ismond Rosen (Ed.), *The Pathology and Treatment of Sexual Deviation: A Methodological Approach*, pp. 351–377. London: Oxford University Press.

EDITORS AND CONTRIBUTORS

Sabina Amiga is a psychotherapist who works in private practice in addition to her work as a forensic psychotherapist at HMP Holloway for over ten years. This work and her background in law and business makes her acutely aware of the changes necessary to turn the justice system into a "just system". Sabina is also trained in eye movement desensitisation processing (EMDR) therapy which she employs in specific incidents of single or more complex trauma. As one of the founders and trustees of Holloway United Therapies (HUT), Sabina continues to work with women who have been involved with the criminal justice system.

Zoe Atkinson works as an art psychotherapist and supervisor in adult mental health services in the NHS and for charities with children and families in schools. Between 2015 and 2016 she co-facilitated the Onyx art therapy group project for women from overseas at HMP Holloway. Zoe has worked as a research associate on varied projects from public health provision for diabetes patients to health needs assessment for people involved in sex work. Zoe's background is in fine art and she has worked as a trapeze artist.

Sophie Benedict is a UKCP registered psychotherapist. She gained her PgDip in Integrative Psychotherapy followed by an MA in Psychotherapy and Counselling. In addition she has completed systemic and mentalisation-based treatment (MBT) training. Sophie spent the first years of her practice at Mind, the mental health charity, before working in HMP Holloway. She has worked for the multi-agency liaison team (MALT), with the NHS and with Women in Prison (WiP). Most recently she has worked with colleagues to set up Holloway United Therapies (HUT) delivering psychological interventions to women affected by the criminal justice system (CJS) in partnership with organisations including Clean Break and Working Chance. Sophie also sees a range of clients through her private practice.

Jessica Collier is an art psychotherapist and clinical supervisor. She worked with female offenders at HMP Holloway until its closure and continues to work with women in the female prison estate. She also works with male offenders at an adapted therapeutic community for men with severe personality disorders within a medium secure hospital. Jessica is a visiting lecturer on the Art Psychotherapy Masters programme at the University of Hertfordshire. She has lectured widely on forensic art psychotherapy and her published work focuses on trauma and unconscious re-enactment. Jessica is the co-convenor of the Forensic Arts Therapies Advisory Group.

Lorna Downing trained as a drama and movement therapist at the Royal Central School of Speech and Drama. She has worked predominantly in forensic services for nearly twenty years. During this time she spent seven years at HMP Holloway running sessions on the health care and vulnerable prisoners unit. Lorna is also a filmmaker and has contributed articles and chapters to academic journals and books, including most recently "Hide my Face. Hear my Voice: Speaking the Unspeakable through Characters and Metaphor" in *Forensic Arts Therapies Anthology of Practice and Research*. Her films include *Inside Out, Kicking Off* and *Friday Night Fever*.

Dr Paola Franciosi was born in Italy where she qualified MD at the Catholic University in Rome and as a psychiatrist at the University of Milan. She moved to London in 1979 to work at St Mary's Hospital and then as a Specialist Registrar at the Addenbrooke's Hospital. Paola worked thereafter as a Consultant at the Abraham Cowley Unit in Chertsey and at HMP Holloway. She is now in private practice in London.

Lorraine Grout is a registered dramatherapist. She completed her final year Masters placement at HMP Holloway where she provided individual and group sessions for women residing on the mental health assessment unit. Previously she has worked in acute adult mental health, specialising in psychotic depression and dementia and with young people with autism spectrum disorder. Lorraine taught drama at HMP YOI Feltham between 2005 and 2010. She is artistic director of Angel Shed Theatre Company and has worked with many organisations working in the criminal justice system including Dance United, Paper Dog Productions and the Irene Taylor Trust. She has also worked artistically with Immediate Theatre, Little Angel Theatre, the Southbank Centre and Centre 404.

Siobhan Lennon is an artist and art psychotherapist. She trained at the University of Hertfordshire, completing her final year Masters placement at HMP Holloway. During this time she developed and co-facilitated the Onyx art therapy group project for female prisoners from overseas. Siobhan continued to work at HMP Holloway in a freelance capacity until its closure. Currently Siobhan works with young offenders within a Central & North West London NHS forensic setting.

Dr Frances Maclennan is a clinical psychologist specialising in forensic populations. In addition to her time at HMP Holloway she has worked in a number of prisons and secure hospitals as well as with community forensic teams and with young offenders in the community. Following the closure of HMP Holloway Frances continues to work across offender services; setting up psychological programmes in secure units. She is a visiting lecturer to clinical psychology trainees and an honorary visiting lecturer to Masters students. Frances has a particular interest in the provision of psychological services to offender populations and has published in this area.

Maureen Mansfield worked for Women in Prison for seven years until the closure of HMP Holloway. In this role she designed, found funding for and managed projects supporting women with "complex needs" in prison. Maureen is currently studying for an MSc in Working with Personality Disorder: Extending Expertise and Enhancing Practice as part of the workforce development under the Offender Personality Disorder Pathway. She is a visiting research fellow at the Harm and Evidence Research Collective: Open University and is on the steering committee of grassroots campaigning group Reclaim Justice Network calling for the radical reduction in the use of the criminal justice system. Maureen is also involved in Reclaim Holloway, a campaigning organisation calling for the public land on the HMP Holloway site to be used for public benefit.

Catherine McCoy is an integrative and focusing-oriented psychotherapist. She worked with female offenders in HMP Holloway for over nine years. She also offers therapy in a drug and alcohol centre and has a private practice. Her inspiration for training as a psychotherapist was ignited while working on the South Asian desk for Amnesty International. Catherine witnessed countless Human Rights violations and realised the need for talking therapies alongside humanitarian aid. She has an interest in homelessness in the UK, having worked for Crisis UK for several years, managing an educational centre in East London for the socially vulnerable. Cathy is a teacher at the London Focusing Institute.

Chrissy Reeves has spent much of her career in the NHS, as a registered mental health nurse and clinical leader, managing large teams of clinical staff through complex change. She ran the health service at HMP Holloway developing it into one recognised as a centre of excellence in its mental health and therapeutic provision. Chrissy manages the London Clinical Network for Health in Justice for NHS England.

Karen Rowe is a psychotherapist, supervisor, academic and consultant with nearly thirty years' experience. She runs a private practice in London. Karen worked at HMP Holloway under Dr Paola Franciosi between 1999 and 2002 while undertaking her specialist training in Forensic Psychotherapy at the Portman Clinic, London.

Pamela Windham Stewart has worked for over twenty years as a psychotherapist in a variety of prisons in southern England, including HMP Wandsworth, where she was the clinical director for Forensic Therapies. In addition she has facilitated therapy groups for mothers and babies in prison as a development of her MA dissertation entitled "Born Inside". Pamela lectures widely and is the founder of the Saturday Forensic Forum which challenges the notion that psychotherapy is of limited use to all but the "worried well". She has a private practice and is a clinical supervisor.

Kimberley Wilson is a chartered psychologist, former chair of the British Psychological Society's Training Committee in Counselling Psychology and currently a governor of the Tavistock & Portman NHS Foundation Trust. Alongside her private practice she led the therapy service at HMP Holloway during its period as a third sector service through to its restructuring as an NHS Primary Care Mental Health provision.

FOREWORD

Estela Welldon

Over the last twenty-five years, the forensic psychotherapy movement has grown by leaps and bounds due to the creative energies of my former students from the seminal course of Forensic Psychotherapy, together with colleagues and friends, who joined the International Association for Forensic Psychotherapy, founded in 1991. These enlightened individuals have pioneered the development of psychotherapeutic and psychoanalytical methods in high-secure institutions, in psychiatric hospitals, and even in community-based organisations, providing psychological treatment, rather than punishment, to those men and women who, due to early trauma, have become forensic patients who have perpetrated acts of criminality.

Sadly, in spite of all these remarkable achievements, surprisingly few colleagues have succeeded in establishing forensic psychotherapy services within the British prison system. Although psychoanalysis and psychotherapists such as John Mackwood, Arthur Hyatt Williams, Margaret Orr and Murray Cox had pioneered prison psychotherapy during the 1950s, 1960s and 1970s, very few have followed in their footsteps. In 2001, one of my former students at the Portman Clinic, Jessica Saunders Williams – a talented dramatherapist – published an edited book entitled *Life within Hidden Walls: Psychotherapy in Prisons*, which chronicled some important projects in the field of prison psychotherapy. In fact, this title held the distinction of being one of the first three titles to appear in the Karnac Books Forensic Psychotherapy Monograph Series, for which I have served as honorary consultant these many years. Regrettably, very little has appeared in print on psychoanalytical approaches to the care of the prisoner in that time.

It pleases me hugely, therefore, that this new book, brilliantly edited by Pamela Windham Stewart and Jessica Collier, has now appeared in print. These passionate colleagues in the forensic therapy field have excelled at recruiting their peers from HMP Holloway and have created a marvellous chronicle of the important work that they have undertaken by working in prison with a psychodynamic lens.

The authors and editors provide us with a magnificent collection of deeply moving stories about life in the prison, about the grim and traumatised backgrounds of the prisoners themselves, and about the ways in which the members of staff have used psychological ideas creatively to bring some relief and compassion and understanding to the inmates.

I feel very proud of my younger colleagues for having assembled such a wonderful addition to our forensic psychotherapy literature and I know that this landmark book on prison psychotherapy will serve as an exciting inspiration to future workers in this important field.

Introduction

Jessica Collier

> Feelings and feelings and feelings. Let me try thinking instead.
> (Lewis, 1961: 32)

The idea to create this book came very quickly, as an almost intuitive response to the shock and anger elicited in us by the sudden decision to close HMP Holloway.

It was a paradox that while serving as an institution of punishment and retribution, the prison simultaneously offered some of the women held within its walls a secure base from which they could begin the arduous work of understanding why they were there. Indeed, HMP Holloway provided a place of personal challenge and discovery to almost everyone who found themselves in its confines for any period of time. When the news came, after years of speculation, that the prison was closing, there was a cry of pain from the crowd listening to the announcement. This was followed by muted silence. As we stood together in the quiet of the chapel, there was a distinct impression that a large and close family had been given news of an untimely and gratuitous death. How to survive this incomprehensible decision became the focus for many of the individuals who had worked in the prison with the women and was responded to in many different ways.

Anecdotally, it seemed that workers who had not been in the prison long, who had other opportunities or who could not manage the uncertainty of waiting to see what would happen, left quickly. Others, principally the prison officers, were mostly treated respectfully and offered new positions in establishments of their choosing. However, the team of professionals who had made up the psychological therapies service in the prison were left in limbo; continuing to provide counselling and therapy to women traumatized by this thoughtless re-enactment of broken attachment and abandonment, while themselves feeling forgotten about, neglected and uncertain about their futures. This mirroring of and working with the women's experience was fundamental to the holding and containment the therapists offered over the years at HMP Holloway. While the women themselves did not have the privilege of choosing whether or when to move, their experience could at least be reflected on within a relationship that was in part based on a shared endeavour to understand and to try thinking as a way of comprehending feelings.

The history of shared psychological exploration in the prison itself is given in this book from the perspective of the professionals who worked there over the years. As rich and varied as this narrative is, it does need to be seen as inherently incomplete. The women's voices are heard only vicariously through the re-telling of the stories they revealed in their therapy sessions or through other working relationships. It is important that when reading the experiences recorded here we keep in mind all that this book cannot communicate; as well as the valuable and hopefully authentic accounts that can be shared. When planning the book we felt we wanted it to elucidate our own perspective. We wanted to write our version of Holloway as a way of surviving and processing our own loss and grief at its closure.

The statistics available on women caught up in the criminal justice system do not make encouraging reading. Over three-quarters of the female prison population are imprisoned for non-violent crimes (Prison Reform Trust, 2017). They are given short sentences that offer no time or opportunity for working on their emotional or mental health needs but often leave them homeless and with very poor prospects. Remaining alive to the possibility of change and the potential for a future worth looking forward to for the prisoners was not easy.

Throughout my time at Holloway I was encouraged to regularly appraise the work I was undertaking using the Clinical Outcome in Routine Evaluation (CORE) questionnaire. This is a list of statements used by clinicians to measure "progress" to which the patient can respond with a prescribed set of answers. These ranged from "not at all" to "most or all the time". Question seventeen asked; "Do you feel optimistic?" I noted over the years that, without exception, the women responded to this question by asking "What does optimistic mean?"

The absence of a way even to describe hope is not surprising given the treatment women offenders have received and continue to receive from society. Forced unthinkingly into a regime designed for men, their identities, opportunities and potential are reduced to almost nothing. Women who are incarcerated often leave vulnerable children behind, frequently in the care system or in families caught in a cycle of trauma, poverty and loss. Left without their mothers, they become the next generation of prisoners. Indeed, prisons are themselves containers for an entire section of the population who accommodate society's own hateful and iniquitous projections. The closure of HMP Holloway, the only women's prison in London and the first to be closed in the capital in over a hundred years, may reflect our desire to push those individuals we deem deserving of punishment further into the margins.

It is a century since women gained partial suffrage and we should not ignore the symbolic importance HMP Holloway played in the history of British feminism, incarcerating as it did a number of activists and suffragettes. These women were treated not as political prisoners but as "common criminals". Harrowing contemporary photographs show exhausted looking individuals tied down and force fed. In stark contrast to this inhumane history, the inspection made immediately prior to the decision to close Holloway was the most positive and encouraging in the prison's recent history. Martin Lomas, the deputy chief inspector of prisons, wrote in the introduction to his report:

> Staff working with the more challenging and complex women in the prison were exceptional … mental health support, including the day care facilities, was excellent … Support for the many women who had been abused was strong … Crucial support around maintaining contact with children and families was much improved and good support was offered to the many women who had been abused … if this is to be our last report on this iconic institution it is undoubtedly one of the best.
> (HM Chief Inspector of Prisons, 2016: 5)

It was in this more empathic climate that HMP Holloway, moving slowly towards a better understanding of emotional and personal needs and a compassionate way of working with often vulnerable and damaged women, was closed.

The following chapters have been written by the individuals who worked with these women; listening, creating, relating and "being with" them as they served their sentences. The authors are mostly not professional writers. Their insights and observations do not put forward ground-breaking new theoretical concepts; although original and innovative initiatives are described. Rather, the aim of this book is to evoke and acknowledge the richness of the many different therapeutic ways of working that took place at HMP Holloway and to mark what has been lost in its untimely ending.

In Chapter One, Maureen Mansfield writes with vigour and passion about the politics of prison, highlighting the organisational preoccupation with figures and data that blinds us to the human stories they measure. Within this discourse she reflects movingly on the resonance between the personal and professional, considering her own motives for working in such a difficult environment and her desire to "save" these damaged women. Maureen's thoughts on the prison as a symbolic mother become more tangible in the following two chapters.

Pamela Windham Stewart (Chapter Two) describes introducing mother and baby groups to the prison and discovering the paradox that HMP Holloway, despite its ostensible position as an institution of punishment, offered a safe and facilitating setting for mothers and their infants to grow together. Pamela thinks about the apparent contradiction that incarceration offers some women a better chance of succeeding as a mother than being overlooked and forgotten in the community. Lorna Downing and Lorraine Grout (Chapter Three) write about dramatherapy in HMP Holloway from the perspective of the pregnant therapist. They discuss the unconscious processes that may have influenced their patient's responses to them as they navigated the risks and dangers to the unborn children they were bringing into the, often toxic, prison atmosphere.

The conversation between Paola Franciosi and Karen Rowe in Chapter Four moves the book into a different area. They examine the difficulties faced by professionals working in an institution that does not understand, on any meaningful level, the tensions and frictions created by the opposing aims of rehabilitation and punishment. Paola and Karen recount the development and fostering of psychoanalytic thinking at HMP Holloway and the ways in which she attempted to link services and people with varying objectives into one body. This dialogue highlights the importance of robust, thoughtful and consistent supervision in supporting therapeutic resilience.

In Chapter Five, Kimberley Wilson offers another perspective on professional and institutional dynamics, addressing the reality of the existence of rivalry and envy between colleagues and within the organization itself. Kimberley proposes this fragmentation might unconsciously replicate externally the prisoner's disorganized internal boundaries and reflects on the challenges these dynamics pose within clinical teams. These conflicts are illustrated further by Chrissy Reeves (Chapter Six), who candidly describes her experience developing the psychological therapies team within the confines of an NHS trust. Chrissy writes with professional authority and personal sadness about the loss of the highly valued service she strived to create and her own perception of feeling discarded; her contribution diminished by an indifferent system.

The next chapters offer detailed case studies to illustrate the complexity of living in prison and the work that can be done to make sense of life in this social microcosm. Siobhan Lennon and Zoe Atkinson (Chapter Seven) use the cycle of life and death as a metaphor for the art psychotherapy group they established for foreign national women at HMP Holloway. Unlike any other space in the prison, the Onyx group provided a communal creative space for individuals who did not share a spoken language or cultural background to communicate and explore their experiences.

In Chapter Eight, Sabina Amiga describes an emotive therapeutic relationship with a woman stuck in prison, many years over tariff, on an Imprisonment for Public Protection (IPP) sentence. She outlines the hopelessness these, now abolished, sentences instil in the prisoners and articulates her own frustration at the injustice she sees in this most cruel and uncertain punishment. Following this, Frances Maclennan and Catherine McCoy (Chapter Nine) detail their group work with a particularly complex woman whose reality – a cycle of incarceration and drug addiction complicated by a severe eating disorder – appeared to be wholly unthinkable. They discuss the ways in which this individual's attempts to deny the pain of her life elicited anxiety and unthinking responses throughout the prison and in the therapist's themselves.

Sophie Benedict (Chapter Ten) then offers a concise personal survey on the effects the closure of Holloway had on the women, the staff and the future of the organizations and therapists that worked for years to help support the prisoners change their lives. Finally, in Chapter Eleven, Jessica Collier introduces a wider cultural perspective on loss and trauma. Encompassing art and social history, she suggests the creative act can be used as a way to mitigate the emotional violence internalized by many women in prison and examines the unconscious re-enactments that further damage already vulnerable people and the resistance shown by society to seeing the brutality in their midst.

The writer and performer A. L. Kennedy suggests that books are "the opposite of death and silence" (Kennedy, 2013). Our intention in bringing these chapters together is to keep alive and amplify the importance of understanding, creativity, thinking and making relationships with those women in society who have been marginalized and condemned in an increasingly hostile political landscape. These individuals have sometimes caused misery to their victims and are not blameless in the lives they lead. Nevertheless, we do them and ourselves a disservice if we do not try to understand what has happened and offer some hope that change is a possibility.

We dedicate this book, with thanks, to the women who fill its pages and who have changed our lives.

REFERENCES

HM Chief Inspector of Prisons (2016) *Report on an Unannounced Inspection of HMP & YOI Holloway*. London: Her Majesty's Inspectorate of Prisons.

Kennedy, A. L. (2013) Home thoughts, and abroad. *The Guardian*, 5 February. Retrieved from www.theguardian.com/books/booksblog/2013/feb/05/al-kennedy-home-thoughts-creative-writing

Lewis, C. S. (1961) *A Grief Observed*. London: Faber & Faber.

Prison Reform Trust (2017) Bromley briefings. Retrieved from www.prisonreformtrust.org.uk/Publications/Factfile

PART I

PRISON AND THE SYMBOLIC MOTHER

CHAPTER ONE

The violence of austerity

Maureen Mansfield

Introduction

HMP Holloway has been entwined with women and gender specific advocacy and reform since its earliest days. Opened in 1852, it became a women-only prison in 1903, following the closure of Newgate Prison a year earlier. Previously the prison had held both men and women together. Mary Russell, Duchess of Bedford, philanthropist and penal reformer, was said to be the person who knew the most about conditions for women in prisons at the time. She was invited to chair the 1919 Committee of Enquiry into Medical Care in Holloway and founded the National Lady Visitor Association – visiting both Holloway and Aylesbury – which "sought to educate them and help them prepare for life after their imprisonment" (Bennett, 2017). Over a century has passed of campaigning for better conditions for women in prison; in HMP Holloway specifically. I worked for the campaigning organisation Women in Prison, in the prison's final years until its closure in 2016. In this chapter I aim to weave my personal experience of HMP Holloway, with the history of the challenge to the prison itself.

A cruel irony of sorts is that despite the long history of reformist and abolitionist efforts centred around the sometimes distressingly harmful Holloway, its closure was not a moment to celebrate. On an otherwise ordinary Wednesday, I was discussing with colleagues the planned proposals to close London's Victorian prisons and build nine new men's prisons, when the closure was announced during the

Government's Autumn Spending Review. I wrongly assumed Holloway, being neither a Victorian prison nor a men's prison, would be unaffected. The news that the prison was to close was monumental; yet the world continued. Of course, aspects of it bubbled up to the public consciousness, but similar to a personal bereavement, many, including myself, wondered how this was not bigger news. The world kept turning as if nothing had changed.

As it happened, the year the decision to close Holloway was made was also personally seismic for me. I lost my sister to breast cancer that January, and my mother, tragically, that September; no longer able to bare her pain enough to stay. Due in part to austerity, there was nothing resembling support for any of us to hold on to. My grand aunt, two uncles and my cat also passed on that year. I experienced the loss of three generations of a family tree; three siblings from a family branch.

The history of organisations in HMP Holloway

Women in Prison (WiP) was established in 1983 by Chris Tchaikovsky, a former prisoner of Holloway, and the academic Pat Carlen. Chris had been in Holloway on minor offences, but during her last stay in the prison in 1974, a woman burned herself to death in a cell. This is surprisingly common and during my time working in the prison women also set fire to themselves amid other desperate actions. Women in Prison was originally a campaigning organisation, born out of a rage against the injustices Tchaikovsky saw there. Alongside Inquest, it emerged with support from a campaigning group called "Radical Alternatives to Prisons" (RAP). Funded by a Christian organisation who were critical of punitive responses and issues of inequalities, they felt strongly that punishment and prison was an inadequate method of achieving behaviour change. As part of their abolitionist organising, RAP produced "Alternatives to Holloway" in 1972. This suggested, as the title implies, alternatives to re-building the prison. Opposing the re-building of the prison, their argument centred around investment in community support, social justice and tackling inequalities. Investment in these areas, they argued, would mean fewer individuals would enter the criminal justice system. Today, Reclaim Holloway is a coalition campaign that has strikingly similar proposals for the public land at Holloway, arguing that it should be used for community support, not sold off to fund more prisons, built further away.

Something about Holloway, its North London location notwithstanding, has always inspired women to organise and campaign for change; to get stuck in practically and provide support. Part of the history of the women's movement is forever connected to the prison. Holloway held political prisoners, most notably, of course, the suffragettes. It also held councillors from Poplar in the 1920s, objectors during both world wars, the Committee of 100, Greenham Common protesters, environmental and animal rights activists, and more recently, women who attempted to fight ISIS with the Kurdish Freedom Party, held under terrorism charges. A less acknowledged contribution to the women's movement, however, is how the prison inspired, or perhaps more accurately, compelled groups of women to organise in response to the conditions within the prison. Women in Prison counts Holloway as its birthplace, alongside others for whom it has made an important contribution including Hibiscus, Women in Secure Hospitals (now Women at WISH), Clean Break, Birth Companions, The Griffins, and more recently, Treasures Foundation and Holloway United Therapies.

Women in Prison's original manifesto illustrates the organisation's understanding of women as a minority in the criminal justice system. It sought to campaign and raise awareness of women as a minority with differing needs in the prison system, as a means to seek to

> unite women of all classes, ethnic backgrounds and sexual orientation in a campaign which, whilst highlighting and attempting to redress the injustices presently suffered by Britain's hitherto neglected women, will also contribute to the wider campaign for democratic control for the criminal justice and penal systems.
>
> (Carlen, 1985: 187)

Written in 1983, WiP's original manifesto contained ten demands for women prisoners, and ten demands for *all* prisoners. It encapsulated a strong desire for prisoners to self-organise and be a collective democratic instrument to subvert and redistribute power universally and democratically. The first point on the manifesto for all prisoners was the democratisation of the criminal and penal justice system in Britain. As such, the origin story of WiP should be understood in ideological terms associated with prison abolition, collective emancipation and solidarity. I believe this is important to frame, in order to contextualise my role within the psychological therapies team at Holloway. Alongside colleagues working with and for the prison and the NHS, I was working within an independent organisation who, from its foundations, challenged the legitimacy of the prison project and had its sights firmly locked on the harms of the state and the systemic institutional harms of imprisonment.

Working in the prison

I worked at Holloway as a mental health manager for WiP, managing the more psychologically informed or complex needs projects of the organisation. At Holloway, the projects were integrated into the psychological therapies team and I attended the weekly referral meeting on behalf of the organisation. During my time with Women in Prison, the complexity and tensions inherent in working for an independent charity in a prison setting gave me an appreciation of what psychoanalytical thinking offers to help understand the unspoken processes at play; both within the work with the women and within teams and organisations. Prison and politics are never far apart, despite the absence of any meaningful public dialogue about what their function is. It would be very difficult to reflect on the work of either WiP or Holloway without mentioning the current socio-political climate and neo-liberalism's impact on the organisation, which was ultimately a predominant factor in Holloway's closure.

During the intervening years between its foundation and the closure of Holloway, WiP expanded and contracted, depending on whatever political and funding narratives were in fashion at the time. Like many other small to medium sized organisations, it changed somewhat in response to the needs of the women and somewhat in response to the organisation's own survival. Having focused on campaigning, Chris and colleagues were continuously approached by women in prison and their families for support. Thus began what is now their core business: supporting women affected by the criminal justice system. While campaigning is still a very important element, the organisations slide towards service delivery mirrors that of many women's organisations established at the time. Having challenged the system from the edges, they have now been co-opted into it, to provide services on behalf of the state. Survival now depends on contracts with government, or privatised companies contracted by the government. Organisations supporting women in the criminal justice system struggle to voice concerns as strongly as they once did.

Consider briefly the scale of intervention that the prison received from community based or women's organisations. In my short time of nearly seven years, WiP alone had fifteen different projects supporting the women in Holloway. Some employed one member of staff, others eight. Funding came from charitable trust funds and some statutory funding streams, which effected a huge change in working culture that I will touch upon later. My contribution was in designing smaller scale, specialist projects focusing on complex needs and therapeutic services responding to trauma and supporting women's engagement; understanding her resistance to cooperating with the system.

Co-option into the system mirrored my own personal experience with the prison. At Holloway, I wavered from initially feeling outside to feeling gradually drawn further inside. How I understood what was happening around me shifted from my interpretation as humanistic counsellor, influenced by phenomenological existentialism, towards a greater appreciation of psychoanalytical thinking. Subtle co-option, was part of Holloway's special way of eliciting more from you, of drawing you in. When the decision to close the prison was made, I doubt anyone accounted for the generosity of spirit Holloway ignited in people, the collective effort involved in making it a better place. My political objections to prisons as a means to solve social problems and my, probably predictable, anti-establishment, anti-authoritarian position matched the women's. Despite that, perhaps even because of it, my attachment and commitment to contributing towards making Holloway "better" was unwavering and it still is as I campaign with Reclaim Holloway.

The prison as mother

The prison captured a part of me, connected to my desire for systemic change; but it also dragged up my unconscious drive in working with women in prison. Both the closure of the prison and the death of my mother brought to the surface the impossible task I had set myself as a child, to "save" my mother, and by extension to strive to "save" the women in prison. This compulsion was as strong as those that brought women into the prison; both the "helper" and the "helped" finding themselves in the same place, for all too similar reasons.

Mothers and mothering was a recurring theme in the prison. Women distraught at being separated from their children might readily be accessible in our minds. However, the sometimes repetitive failure of the mothers of the women in prison to protect or believe their daughters was emotionally annihilating. Inconsistent care, abuse and neglect create early attachments and patterns that can result in mistrust and a lack of "reflective functioning", defined as the capacity to understand your own thoughts and feelings and the intentions of others (Bateman and Fonagy, 2004). I heard shocking stories of women being prostituted by their mothers, which I experienced alongside their desire for a better relationship; to get what their mothers could never give them. This desire was so strong that repeated attempts to support some on release, meeting the same woman at the prison gates five, ten or fifteen times, would result in her inevitable return to her mother. This in turn brought along the crack addictions and sex working and the return to prison. In a way, we were somehow together in prison because of our mothers. This observation is not to attribute blame to mothers, but to understand the strong dynamics at play. Returning to prison was perpetuated as a result of the failure of this wish for containment, a longing to be held and contained. Prison can be seen as a stand in for mother, with the women "forcing their way in so violently, they usually find there is no longer an 'inside' that can hold them; the urge to get inside becomes even more urgent" (Adlam and Scanlon in Aiyegbusi, 2009: 129). Those women usually found themselves even deeper in the prison system, spending some time in the care and separation unit, or health care unit. Women with disrupted attachments have an increased risk of externalising behavioural problems, especially when other social risk factors are present (Belsky and Fearon, 2002). These contribute to repeated transgenerational patterns of difficult adult relationships, disrupted attachments (Yakeley, 2010) and maternal abuse and neglect (Motz, 2008). A difficult maternal relationship is a greater predictor of offending in women than men. While the truth is that prison can never be a home, it helps us understand why the closure of HMP Holloway felt so monumental. It also helps in understanding the managerial problems in forensic institutions and the dependency inherent in these systems (Adshead, 2002; Barrett, 2011).

I felt the loss of Holloway, as a container, and as the "Concrete Mother" (Motz, 2008), acutely, and perhaps on behalf of the generations of women and campaigners gone before. There is profound internal anxiety concerning psychic survival (Adlam and Scanlon in Aiyegbusi, 2009) located in dedicated forensic services. Those working within the complex system feel entwined with the organisation. The organisational is also the personal. Structures and policies are bound up with the inner emotional lives of those working within them, while simultaneously trying to change them (Armstrong, 1991). In order to be able to offer "healthy" psychological interventions, the perpetual loss, absences and abandonment in the "mind" of any team has to be acknowledged. The organisations associated with Holloway underwent a similar negation of their traumatic experiences as that of the women. In writing I have come to recognise that the closure, as it interweaved around my own losses, has meant I have given myself another impossible task to replace saving my own mother: to keep Holloway alive. Or at least try to make it better understood. This mirrors the litanies of unrecognised and unspoken losses that bring women to prison, as they used their own lives and bodies as memorials in the absence of acknowledgement of their loss and abandonment. Those affected carry "the fear that we will forget as well as be forgotten and lose what has been of value" (Salzberger-Wittenberg, 1999).

The particular character of any organisation is a reflection of the client group and workers and may get in the way of healthy functioning (Stokoe, 2011). An organisation founded by a former prisoner, which at one point only employed women with personal experience of imprisonment, WiP are particularly vulnerable to operating in a fragmented mode. Set up to work with women traumatised and "dismembered" from society, it becomes itself traumatised and dismembered as staff try to deal with the anxiety arising from the failed dependence within the system, alongside their own drive towards the work. Exposed to raw, unprocessed projections and organised around the victim/perpetrator split in the first instance, one is vulnerable to acting out these dynamics and engaging in sado-masochistic behaviour if not provided with opportunities to understand the unconscious processes that support this sort of painful interpersonal relating (Aiyegbusi, 2009).

Autonomy and independence

Just as the women found themselves in deep custody, in the bowels of the prison, I too found myself working with longer sentenced women, entrenched and embattled. The task for WiP when working with these women who did not "engage" was to use our independence to help translate the system. To help women see the matrix ahead of them; to help them to understand as early as possible, the challenges they faced from "the system". We wanted to support them in understanding what was and is in their control and what wasn't and where to place their attention and energy. While understandable, the systemic injustices they might feel would not help with their own plans for being released. Being a campaigning organisation has helped the women to hand over some of their frustrations, to support them to move beyond the desire to resist the brutal punitive system using the only tool available to them: their own progress. Helping women navigate a course through, to emotionally manage the hurdles, challenges and knock-backs they faced without sabotaging themselves in an environment and system that sets them up to fail is the primary task.

Women are expected and encouraged to take responsibility for their offending, their histories and their current problems. Hannah-Moffat (2006) suggests women are not regarded as victims of social circumstance, but as inept individuals who are powerless at avoiding crime, discrimination and unemployment. Circumstances that lead to criminal behaviour and imprisonment are deemed to be *their choice.* They are, therefore, expected to have the capacity to make different choices. Both problem and solution are located within them *as individuals.* Programmes often follow individualising and compartmentalising needs, sometimes failing to appreciate how gender operates. A vulnerable woman preparing and attempting to use the support available is a complex negotiation working in prison. While engagement through voluntary volition is optimal for both psychotherapy, and organisations like WiP, success is only really attainable if her intent, desire and will make it possible; if not from the start then at least nurtured proactively to get there.

The importance of the relationship

This task is somewhat achievable with the right support and good working relationships within the institution. I worked with a woman I will call Catherine, who was over her sentence tariff by decades. When we started she was full of righteous rage about the failures of the prison that repeatedly let her down beyond any point of return; the damage irreparable. She presented to me a very rational case as to why she could no longer be in prison and why she thought it detrimental to her health and wellbeing. Catherine wanted to move to another institution to complete an "Accredited Offender Behaviour" programme. However, her probation and mental health team would not consider a transfer until she "engaged" with their support. Catherine was on an indeterminate sentence and would not be seen as making progress by the parole board unless she had completed this or other accredited programmes. She was trapped in an impossible, Kafkaesque task. Her probation team were not supportive of her move without the mental health team's approval and the psychiatrist's agreement.

My role was to support Catherine to understand the process and help her to show some level of "engagement". We met weekly to gain trust, initially with another colleague. On one level I did this to ensure I was not colluding with Catherine in hating the prison, but it is also emotionally demanding working with women decades over tariff and I too wanted support. It's not the women that are demanding, as such, it's the frustration that mainlines into your veins when trying to make some impact into this maddening matrix. Using the independence and powerlessness of WiP is perhaps the most powerful factor in building relationships with women who struggle to "engage" with the system. Our lack of authority allows us to listen in a way that we could not if we represented the prison, or another powerful force. This is not about the denigration of professionals, but about helping women like Catherine to communicate in a way that might be more productive; helping her realise that she did have options and control, albeit restricted. Eventually she agreed to come to one of WiP's groups called "Choices". We outlined where she was in the system, and told her what we had already seen; that there are women in prison on even longer sentences, with the same anger and hatred of the prison system. Using their own progress to punish the people around them, much like Catherine was doing, had only got them further away from any prospect of release. Catherine had some options in this scenario, whether she felt them or not. Whether her anger was well founded was not relevant to her progress out of the prison. She needed to channel her passion and anger. If this can be harnessed, it's much more productive to work with than someone vacantly repeating messages of compliance.

Catherine struggled with group work, challenged even by the thought of it. She rarely left her landing as she did not feel safe anywhere. However, as an intelligent and incidentally talented woman, she could see that unless she proved she could engage with group work, she was unlikely to be transferred to another prison to complete a group work-based programme. Only by asking that she turn up and assuring her that I would make no further demands was Catherine able to attend. She sat literally turned away from the rest of the women and remained that way for the full session. I met with her afterwards and we discussed what was going on for her, how she felt about the group and her impact on the other women. We made a plan for week two: turn up.

Arriving to the second group required a herculean effort, but once Catherine made it there I felt that perhaps, something could really be achieved. Once again she sat through the group, this time facing the other women, her body no longer turned away but not yet communicating verbally. By week eight, Catherine was sitting on the floor with the other women, chatting about their shared challenges while making cards to send to her family. She had successfully completed the group and so could evidence her willingness to engage. Along with meeting weekly with Catherine I regularly spoke with her probation and mental health team about the plan we were working on. I attended multi-disciplinary meetings, encouraging her to attend, which she did. I acknowledged that my approach could only work because I was operating from a certain position in, or rather outside, the system. We were all able to depersonalise what was going on.

Catherine's mental health team felt that "holding on" to her rather than "rejecting" her was the most therapeutically valuable thing to do and while she profoundly disagreed with them, she came to recognise their fears. Here we arrive at one of the contradictions of therapeutically supporting women in prison. Catherine was not in Holloway to receive therapy or mental health support. She was in Holloway to serve a prison sentence for a crime of violence. To serve time until the system decided she no longer posed a risk. She might be able to prove this by engaging with therapy or mental health support at Holloway, but an accredited behaviour programme would probably have better traction with the parole board. While Holloway held on to her on "therapeutic" grounds, attempting to contain her emotionally, they were simultaneously adversely affecting her movement through the system.

After more than a year of working together Catherine was transferred to another prison to complete the programme. Following this she was successfully released into the community where she has remained for a number of years. It helped that WiP provided advocacy outside the prison, so she could continue to receive on-going support. It also helped that I had a relationship with the probation team and mental health team, built up over years, that could withstand the splitting and projecting as it arose, and that I was secure in my membership of the psychological therapies team. Furthermore, Catherine found a way to embrace and overcome her fears. She could perhaps, speak more freely about these as I was not in a position to deny or grant her freedom. What I offered was just a supporting frame to the real element required. The work, persistence, endurance, bravery and risk she was willing to take to move forward. She did this with great success.

The closure of Holloway

The Corston Report, published in 2007, was a response to the drastically high level of self-inflicted deaths at HMP Styal. Intervening years saw initial improvements in services and a reduction in the number of deaths. Sadly, ten years later in 2017, and in my view not unconnected with the decision to close Holloway, there were twenty-two deaths of women in the custody of prisons in England.

Holloway, a problematic institution right up until the end, was a contradiction even as it was closing. Despite wanting to see a radical reduction of the women's prison estate, neither Baroness Corston nor WiP could wholeheartedly support the decision. This was particularly strongly felt in the absence of any strategies for addressing the problem faced by prisons, the organisations that support the women and the women themselves. As the prison was winding down following the closure announcement, Holloway had a positive inspectorate report published including the admission from the inspectorate that it was one of the best. That the decision to finally close the prison was made at a time when it was arguably at its healthiest is perhaps the cruellest of all Holloway's ironies. Closed not because of campaigns to improve conditions, or reduce the women's prison population; Holloway Prison was closed to sell off high-value public land to purportedly finance the building of new, larger prisons much further away. This removed from sight and public consciousness the confrontation of what we as a society have chosen to do in defence of our own sense of "belonging". In my own personal ambivalence and reaction to this decision alone we can observe a microcosm of the challenges of trying to work within a system, while also wishing to bring about its end.

Attention is our most valuable resource; operating under new "payment by results" contracts has meant a violent re-focusing of attention away from relationships and towards numbers. Having to complete an oppressive amount of monitoring and evaluation steals time and needs space to think. Without this, we are locked into responding to the ever-increasing demands that the machine be fed, starving service quality, organisational integrity and resistance. The language used has changed, and staff sense they are being conditioned; internalising the surveillance and adapting in response. Thinking becomes impossible. Just as security concerns within prisons often trump therapeutic issues, risk of data breach trumps the person. Data is arguably more safely contained than the women it has been stripped from. Files are password encrypted, paper files stored behind locked safes whose keys are stored in locked cabinets, within offices that have two locks on the doors. We have moved from having strong working theories about a system – but data deemed not robust enough to "evidence" it – to an excessive level of data, all of which is there to prop up weak theory.

There has been an incontestable shift from time spent nurturing relationships to time spent nurturing databases. Being told what counts as a success by the terms of funding contracts frequently denies lived reality for both the woman and those working with her. This incongruity affects high levels of stress and frequent burnout for staff. To survive some comply, but may find it is not uncommon to start resenting colleagues and the women for not making the right kind of progress. The impact on women is far more chilling, as they are violently denied basic care and services for "intentionality" and not "engaging". The women who ultimately end up in prison, and I am using the phrase "ultimately end up" to highlight that there was a path that got them there; are routinely discharged from community based services due to *their* failure to *engage*. They are told by housing authorities that they no longer have a duty of care to them as they "intentionally" made themselves homeless by being sent to prison. The safety and containment that prison can afford really does become the only support or safety available; there is nothing left to hold on to for these women in the community. Where services and support might previously have existed they now face a minefield of referral agencies referring women on into the void with competitive zeal.

Often accompanying this drive towards improving monitoring and data collection is the challenge "what is the 'evidence-base' for your intervention?" a challenge often levied against long term psychotherapy. It is a phrase that Doctor (2010: 1) says "supplies a sense of authority in situations where uncertainty is a daily companion, anxiety is high and needs are pressing". This fits the bill for the justice system. Anything that does not fit neatly and rationally into the framework seems unreasonable, if not reprehensible. He proposes that a more useful inquiry would be whether it is "experience-based". In the decision to close the prison neither the experience of women or the professionals working in Holloway was given anything near recognition.

I have seen first-hand the machinations of delivering services under these conditions; co-opting and oppressing organisations and individuals, silencing dissent and ultimately pushing women further away. The pervasive myth of the individual and the focus on "choice and responsibility" causes untold damage to women in the prison system. The focus on providing a solid "evidence-base", drawn from lengthy monitoring processes results not in conclusive proof of the efficacy of the services to improve the lives of the women being helped, but to ensure payment. This results in increased deaths of vulnerable people and the destruction of public helping institutions.

One such loss is the closure of HMP Holloway; the land to be sold at profit to continue prisons. We misunderstand this cycle so badly that reform brings us back full circle to the idea that new prisons can be offered as the solution to old prisons. Unless we start thinking differently, someone will be writing in another hundred years about an old prison with sadness and affection: an institution that caused generations of harm and never quite worked, despite the willingness of people who tried their best. Holloway was closed in order to obtain money to build another prison. It seems we are destined to repeat the same mistakes until we can understand them.

Moving on

In March 2017, I attended a function in the House of Lords celebrating the tenth year of Baroness Jean Corston's report on women in prison. There in the House of Lords, I ran into Catherine and we recollected the day we first met at Holloway. Looking out onto the River Thames as it flowed by, we exchanged pictures of our pet cats and reflected on how far we had come since that first meeting. Catherine was no longer in prison. Holloway was no longer open. I was no longer working for Women in Prison and in my mind, unsaid, I knew I was no longer trying to save my mother.

The psychiatrist who had been rightly concerned that Catherine would not be able to manage the transition, was also at the event. Eating canapes and discussing the usual theme of reform, I wondered if anyone can ever really understand anything they are immersed in while they are immersed in it. Perhaps it is really only with time, distance and reflection that things come into focus.

REFERENCES

Adshead, G. (2002). Three degrees of security: Attachment and forensic settings institutions. *Criminal Behaviour and Mental Health*, 12, S31–S45.
Aiyegbusi, A. (2009). The dynamics of difference. In A. Aiyegbusi (eds), *Therapeutic relationships with offenders: An introduction to the psycho dynamics of forensic mental health nursing*. London: Jessica Kingsley.

Armstrong, D. (1991). The institution in the mind: Reflections on the relation of psychoanalysis to work with institutions. Retrieved from www.human-nature.com/group/chap6.html

Barrett, J. (2011). Sustainable organizations in health and social care: Developing a "team mind". In A. Rubitel and D. Reiss (eds), *Containment in the community: Supportive frameworks for thinking about antisocial behaviour and mental health*. London: Karnac Books.

Bateman, A. W., & Fonagy, P. (2004). *Psychotherapy for borderline personality disorder: Mentalization based treatment*. Oxford: Oxford University Press.

Belsky, J., & Fearon, R. M. P. (2002). Infant-mother attachment security, contextual risk, and early development: A moderational analysis. *Development and Psychopathology*, 14, 293–310.

Bennett, R. (2017). Identifying & advocating for women's health: The Duchess of Bedford's 1919 committee of enquiry into medical care in Holloway Prison. https://histprisonhealth.com/policy-events/inside-reform/background/holloway-womens-prison

Carlen, P. (1985). *Criminal women*. Cambridge: Polity Press.

Doctor, R. (2010). *Murder*. London: Karnac Books.

Hannah-Moffat, K. (2006). Pandora's box: Risk/need and gender responsive corrections. *Criminology & Public Policy*, 5(1), 183–192. DOI: 10.1111/j.1745-9133.2006.00113.x.

Motz, A. (2008). *The psychology of female violence: Crimes against the body*. Hove: Routledge.

Salzberger-Wittenberg, I. (1999). Different kinds of endings. in I. Salzberger-Wittenberg, G. Williams, and E. Osborne (eds), *The emotional experience of teaching and learning*. London: Karnac Books.

Scanlon, C., and Adlam, J. (2009). Nursing dangerousness, dangerous nursing and the spaces in between: Learning to live with uncertainties. In A. Aiyegbusi and J. Clarke (eds), *Relationships with offenders: An Introduction to the psychodynamics of forensic mental health nursing* (pp. 127–142). London: Jessica Kingsley.

Stokoe, P. (2011). The healthy and the unhealthy organization: How can we help teams to remain effective? In A. Rubitel and D. Reiss (eds), *Containment in the community: Supportive frameworks for thinking about antisocial behaviour and mental health*. London: Karnac Books.

Yakeley, J. (2010). *Working with violence: A contemporary psychoanalytic approach*. London: Palgrave Macmillan.

CHAPTER TWO

Twenty years in prison

Reflections on the birth of the Born Inside project and psychotherapy in HMP Holloway

Pamela Windham Stewart

In this chapter, I reflect on my twenty years in HMP Holloway where I began work carrying out an infant observation and left as a psychotherapist working not only with pregnant inmates, mothers and babies but also a wide range of offenders convicted of very violent crimes. This work made me wonder if, having explored the childhoods of the women, was there ever a time when they had the luxury of making more hopeful and creative choices that could have kept them from coming to prison to serve long sentences. Were their choices any more than the "sum of all the choices gone before" (Didion, 1963: 31)

Infant observation goes to prison

At the end of my Master of Arts (MA) in Observational Studies in 1996, the time came to present the MA dissertation proposal. The practice of infant observation was developed by the psychoanalyst Ester Bick in 1948 and became part of the training for students studying to become child psychoanalytic child psychotherapists (Bick, 1964). By the 1970s, infant observation had developed into a course suitable for a larger group of professions.

This is how the observation works. Ideally before the baby is born the observer finds a mother willing for the observer to come at a regular time each week for one hour over two years to stay with and observe the baby. There is a parallel here with psychoanalytic work. The observer pays close attention to the feelings of being with the baby and does not take notes or give opinions or information to the mother or primary care giver. When the session ends, the observer reflects on the session writing up careful notes on the observation and later presenting these notes for further discussion in supervision. Often the observer struggles with the desperate feelings evoked by an often anxious mother and a tiny, vulnerable baby in addition to her own anxiety about getting it "right". From the outset managing one's own uncertainties are central to the observation. It takes time to realise that doing "nothing" is in fact doing a great deal.

Infant observations can be a challenging process. "It is a great equaliser. It strips away much of what we thought we knew and exposes the ignorance and prejudice in each of us" (Reed, 1997: 2). For many and certainly for me, becoming a thoughtful observer was a huge struggle. It was very difficult staying with the experience and not flying into action through advice giving or chatting. Slowly and over time this profound experience trained me to feel and think about both mother and baby. The generous mother who agreed to help me was a well-educated middle class married woman in her early thirties. She was reliable and learned over time not to ask my opinion but allowed me the freedom to get on with the task of observing. I am eternally grateful to her and mothers like her who allow students entry into this delicate and intricate world of emerging relationships. During the two years of observation, I struggled with the theoretical emphasis on the internal world of the baby often wondering also about the external world in which the baby was living. "My" observed baby lived in a thoughtful environment where her physical and emotional needs were considered important. I began to wonder about the impact and outcome of a deprived external environment on the mother and baby relationship. We now take as given that the relationship with the mother is central to the future development of the baby (and in many cases the mother). But I was curious to observe the growth of the mother–baby bond in a less facilitating environment. I assumed a less thoughtful, physically impoverished environment would be detrimental to growth and development of the infant. I was beginning to understand how anxiety inhibits a mother's capacity to hold the baby in mind. Might a mother, deprived on both internal and external levels be depressed and less able to respond to her baby?

Where might I find such an environment? Prison sprang to mind, not only as a metaphor for depression but the actual, concrete building.

Traditionally people attempt to escape from prison – my task was to get into one. The thought that there might be a connection between social institutions and the mental health of mothers led to my dissertation proposal which I presented in November 1995. Overcoming my feelings of nervousness and worthlessness, I presented my proposal which I called "Born Inside". My initial idea was to observe a mother and baby in a difficult setting – a prison. When I spoke the room was silent, you could hear a pin drop. The proposal was accepted.

Next step was to write to HMP Holloway with cautious optimism and, paradoxically, also almost hoping at times that I would hear nothing back. My initial research revealed that HMP Holloway was the largest women's prison in Europe. I also learned that the UK has the largest prison population of any country in western Europe. After a long wait, I was invited to HMP Holloway to discuss my proposal in the spring of 1996. As I walked into the prison, the Chief Inspector of Prisons, David Ramsbotham, was walking out. He had refused to continue the inspection. He began speaking to the press gathered by the prison's entrance. With eloquent precision he expressed his horror at the conditions in which the women were held. Underneath his dignified military bearing he appeared to be seething.

Walking past Lord Ramsbotham and the television cameras, I entered HMP Holloway for the first time. At the reception area, I presented myself to the officer behind the bullet-proof window. Handing over my American passport for identification I then sat down to wait for my meeting. I had no idea what to expect. Hanging on the wall was a dazzling, huge copy of Klimt's *The Kiss*. The swirling coils of gold and the tenderness of the embrace shone out in contrast to the barren, brutal waiting room and the media mayhem erupting outside.

A male, uniformed prison officer approached me and requested that I come with him to the mother and baby unit (MBU), which was located on the fourth floor of the prison. I apologised for being very early. In a relaxed voice, at odds with his uniform, he said that was fine. In fact, he said, if I wished, I could sit in on the admissions board which assessed pregnant women's suitability for a precious place on the twelve-cell MBU. There I would later learn about the strict criteria for acceptance onto the unit. As we walked up the stairs the inside of the prison looked and felt like a bunker with heavy concrete walls and huge metal barred gates which required a lot of unlocking and then locking. By this point I was slightly surprised by the friendly and accepting welcome extended to me by the officers I was introduced to as I joined the mother and baby admissions board. Over the next hour I observed the board as two, frightened young pregnant women were interviewed individually for a place on the unit. Both were in their last weeks of pregnancy. Each silent and anxious woman faced the huge uncertainty of whether she would be able to keep her baby with her in prison whilst serving a prison sentence. I could not imagine how this must feel at any time, particularly in the final, emotional days before giving birth at a hospital near the prison, alone, attended by strangers and, at that time, handcuffed to the labour bed.

After observing these tense interviews, it was my turn. The governor of the unit enquired about my research. I spoke at length about the observation model of mothers and babies and my interest in considering the impact of imprisonment on the mother and baby relationship. My hypothesis (i.e. that prison represented a place of great emotional insecurity and anxiety for the mothers which would impede close relating between mother and baby) I kept to myself. Indeed, Lord Ramsbotham's refusal to inspect fuelled my assumption that prison was an unacceptable environment for anyone in civilised society, never mind a mother and baby. The governor listened and smiled at me but did not give much away other than to state that the prison was regularly swamped with requests from researchers. With a sigh I felt my heart start sinking. He firmly emphasised that the unit was the "home of mothers at very sensitive periods of their life. This is their home. We do not want them to feel like animals in the zoo." I completely agreed with him. Referring to the baby observation model, I said that in my experience, meeting regularly once a week could be very supportive to a mother, particularly one who did not have family around her. To my absolute amazement he agreed with me. What day would I like to start, he asked. My lower jaw hit the floor with disbelief. I will never know how he made his decision or why it was so easy. Given the passage of twenty years I know this would be impossible now. But after two hours I was on my way to observe a mother and baby weekly in the largest female prison in Europe. As I left the prison, escorted by an officer, I wondered what on earth I had let myself into as iron gates clanged behind me.

Getting on: HMP Holloway in 1996

On my first day of observations, I needed to establish a connection between a mother and baby. I discussed this with the officer in charge. I knew my project would require the support and interest of the officers on duty in the MBU – I was keen to involve them. I enquired about potential mothers who would be willing to meet with me each week and help me with my research. The officer introduced me to Abigail who had a two-week-old son, Alfie. I presented my idea of observing and getting to know her and Alfie through weekly visits. Abigail stated that she would like having someone visit her as her family were from the north and she was very lonely. I explained that I would come and see them for an hour, that I was interested in seeing how they were both getting on. I explained that I was not there to judge them, give advice or advocate for them in any way. Abigail smiled and said it would just be "nice to see someone who is not an officer or another prisoner". I replied that I would see her next week. At the same time Abigail smiled, glanced down at Alfie and then nodded back to me. Abigail looked very small and slightly stranded. Alfie slept the entire time. I left their tiny cell with the lidless toilet in the corner, relieved, thinking that my project was on its way. I would soon learn that nothing goes smoothly in prison.

The following week when I arrived, eager to graft the observational model onto the MBU, Abigail and Alfie were gone. Gone. They had suddenly been transferred to another prison far from London. I felt the project begin to crumble. Looking at her cell and seeing a different mother and baby there, I wondered if I should ask this mother and repeat the whole process again. An inner voice steered me away from making a hasty decision. Instead I walked back to the unit office with the intention to speak to an officer. On my way, I noticed the association room was full of the other mothers and their babies talking and sitting together. I had an idea. What if I did an observation of the unit? This way no mother would be left out. When one mother and baby left, the group would re-configure but continue. Taking a deep breath I entered the association room and started talking with the mothers who for some reason seemed happy to speak with me. Born Inside was born.

HMP Holloway 1996–1998

During the initial two years of observing mothers and babies, the general British female population doubled, although the crime rate did not. Nonetheless the crime statistics were staggering. Judges were increasingly handing more custodial sentences to women. The total capacity at HMP Holloway was approximately five hundred women. However, at times, the prison expanded to nearly six hundred.

Approximately three thousand women would pass through at a cost of around £30,000 per woman per year. Foreign national women (approximately 20%) suffered the additional agony of being detained far from their countries of origin and were often unable to speak English. During this period most of them were drugs mules, the foot soldiers of the expanding international drugs trade. Approximately half of the women were on remand and were facing a lengthy wait before going on trial.

The imprisonment of women has far-reaching implications for herself and her family. The impact of imprisonment on female offenders has been well documented in prior research (Murray, 2005; Douglas, Plugge and Fitzpatrick, 2009; Foster, 2012; MacDonald, 2013). Studies have suggested that children of parents in prison are twice as likely to experience mental health difficulties and experience difficulties in school settings and are three times more likely to engage in criminal behaviours (Barnado's, 2017). Imprisonment can also exacerbate socio-economic disadvantage (Prison Reform Trust, 2017) and has been associated to the likelihood of mental health difficulties (Prison Reform Trust, 2015; Fazel, Hayes, Bartellas, Clerici and Trestman, 2016). Forty-six per cent of women are estimated to have attempted suicide and nearly half of the female prison population present with mental health problems (Independent, 2017). Statistics provide one way of trying to understand prisoners. However the narratives about the mothers and babies residing in prison settings may provide another way understanding of life behind bars.

Knowing the backgrounds of women in prison can stir up a lot of emotion in people working with them. Anguished concern for children left behind is a very emotional concern for professions. Most of the women's crimes are impulsive. To say that the mothers should have thought about the impact of their behaviour on their children demonstrates ignorance. Society does not give enough thought to the lives and social conditions female prisoners experience before offending. These damaged women rarely have a chance to develop insight and agency. Where were their emotional and social supports required for the development of insight? Why it is that children failed by society – emotionally, physically and academically – grow up to be punished for society's failures of them? After all these years my anger and rage continue to grow. Anger with the prison system is misdirected and a moral diversion. Prison is a social institution and as such we, as a society, are responsible, not only for the way prisoners are treated but also for the conditions which produce them in the first place. To understand the childhoods of most of the prison population is easy. Read the Charles Dickens classic,

Oliver Twist. Skip the happy ending. These strong emotions fuel forensic work but must be kept in mind and not acted out when working in prisons.

Getting going: observational material

Prison is an institution full of power dynamics and complexity (Foucault, 1977). To add to the complexity of observing in a prison, there are many times when it functions creatively encouraging and facilitating growth. Observing would have been easier if the prison had been a consistently thought-blocking institution staffed by unthinking officers. Much more intricate than media reports or popular prison films and TV shows indicate, my proposal would never have been accepted if the prison staff had been incapable of thought. Perhaps it is society at large that fails to understand and think about the people we imprison. How much does society need to have a group of people that we can send away for being "bad"? Strout (2016: 95) summed up these sentiments by her interest in

> how we find ways to feel superior to another person, another group of people. It happens everywhere, and all the time. Whatever we call it ... it is the lowest part of who we are this need to find someone else to put down.

I think this is the function prison performs for society; that means you and me.

My weekly observations started. I would come at the agreed and reliable time and see what happened on the unit. What follows are vignettes from work with Gabrielle, one of the mothers who agreed to talk with me. Here are three brief excerpts of observing her and her son on the unit.

July 1997: mother, Gabrielle (nineteen years) and son, Luther (seven months)

Coming onto the unit I saw Gabrielle and Luther. Convicted of passing drugs to her partner (Luther's father) on a visit to see the father in prison Gabrielle gave birth to Luther while in Holloway. In February when I first met Gabrielle and Luther they had both appeared frightened and withdrawn in the group. Gabrielle also had a daughter in the community. When I first saw Gabrielle, her skin was raw and ravaged by acne. However, by July both she and Luther appeared well-cared for, as if their skin had been freshly washed and ironed. I found them in the association room with a baby named Cinnamon. It was a few minutes before the mother and baby group was scheduled to begin. Gabrielle was mopping the association room floor, getting it ready for the group.

Cinnamon crawled over to Luther who was strapped in his baby seat. He was in the seat, so his mother could do her cleaning. The thin prison windows were open infusing the room with summer warmth and light. Beaming at Cinnamon, Luther checked his mother's face. Gabrielle made confirming, clicking sounds as both babies watched her. "Shall I set you free?" Gabrielle asked Luther. Leaning down Gabrielle opened the straps allowing Luther to crawl over to Cinnamon who was tapping her feet and waving a small toy in excitement. "Look at him go", laughed his mother.

After their months together in prison, both mother and son looked completely different. Gabrielle now had a paid prison job cleaning on the unit. She had attended a bereavement course run by the prison and said she had been able to mourn the death of her father. Luther's diet was watched by the health visitor who had assisted Gabrielle in cooking for him. Gabrielle had spoken about her mother's many absences from home when Gabrielle was little. Now Gabrielle realised the absences were a result of her own mother's time in Holloway. She said that she had passed her mother leaving prison when she and Luther returned from hospital. For once, Gabrielle said, "I know where my mother is today. She is in prison." The safety Gabrielle felt on the MBU, the routine, regular food and personal safety had given her a sense of security which seemed to make possible a relationship of mutual responsiveness with her now flourishing and playful son.

August 1997

Returning from his swim in the prison pool the summer light danced on Luther's damp skin. He and his mother walked towards me. Both dressed in white. Placing Luther in a baby walker she said to both of us that she was going to make his lunch. With a happy shriek Luther pushed hard with his legs propelling the walker down the long prison corridor.

Returning, Gabrielle called out "Luther" and he raced back in the walker. Carefully placing his bottle where he could see it she put Luther in the high chair. She acknowledged that Luther "could have a drink in a minute, I just want to make sure that your food is not too hot". Luther seemed to understand because he looked at his bottle with a smile and then looked back at this mother who was sitting in front of him. Returning his smile, Gabrielle tasted the food with happy, smacking noises and said it was fine. Carefully she placed a small blue plastic spoon in his already opened mouth. With grace she turned the spoon and then wiped his bottom lip with a cloth she had brought with her. Thumping his legs with delight Luther nodded at me, as if making conversation.

October 1997

When Gabrielle had entered prison the previous winter I noticed large warts on the inside of her arms. Now many months later the hospital appointment for the wart removal arrived. It arrived just as her release date approached. In order to have the operation Gabrielle had to leave Luther with the prison staff. Both were upset and tearful about the separation.

During the operation her arms began to bleed and she was told that the wart removal would have to be completed once she was released. With more thought and planning this operation could have taken place earlier in her sentence when she would have had the support of the prison staff in caring for Luther. The further postponement meant that she could not use her arms to hold anything, particularly her son. Sadly, days later Gabrielle was released from prison literally unable to hold her baby, in body or mind. At the same time Luther developed very severe conjunctivitis.

In his cell Luther stood bleary-eyed and alone. He was being kept away from the other babies because of the infection. He looked hot and miserable with a crusty red face and oozing eyes. Gloomily he caught my eye. His dirty dummy dangled from the corner of his mouth. A prison officer passing by stopped and we looked at Luther together. The officer told me that last night she had given Luther a bath because Gabrielle could not hold him. He loved it, she said. We smiled at him, but he looked away. The officer said that she could tell that it had been ages since he had been washed because he was very grubby and his bottom was red and very sore.

Looking at Luther together the officer and I talked about how much he and his mother loved going swimming and how well they had been during the last few months. Now Luther looked like a melting candle. His smell filled the room. It seemed to come from every pore; not just the dirty, pungent nappy smell. Much worse, from the top of his head down to his feet came a smell of decay. Walking down the hall we could hear Gabrielle calling "Luther, where is my sexy boy?" Coming into the cell she flopped on her bed and pulled Luther limply across her lap.

Thoughts

Confronted with the looming loss of their home/prison, Gabrielle seemed to lose hold of her son. Anxiety appeared to overcome this once competent mother and Luther's skin seemed to erupt as a result. Her gleaming son was now reduced to a thing, a "sexy boy" – no longer her baby. Unable to understand Luther's liquefying state, Gabrielle treated the child as a sexualised and inappropriate source of comfort for herself (Welldon, 2000). Time and time again, I witness the collapse of healthy relating as the release approaches and both mother and baby become helpless strangers to each other.

With Gabrielle's departure it was clear to me that my early hypothesis that mothers and babies could not thrive in a prison had collapsed. Gabrielle and Luther came alive in what I had assumed would be a hostile environment. The difficulty facing them was not having been in prison. The problem ahead was going home. I continue to witness this in the mother and baby groups, and by now have worked with over four hundred mothers.

First closure: closing of the Holloway Mother and Baby Unit, 2014

When I first crossed the prison threshold in 1996 rumour had it that HMP Holloway was closing. From time to time, the press or a staff member would resurrect the idea. However, no one took any of this to heart. Looking back maybe I missed signs of change. Suddenly in October 2014, the closure of the MBU was announced. The unit would be recommissioned for women preparing for release. Resident mothers were quickly transferred to prisons outside of London. Their home on the unit, their relationships with each other and the staff, all came to an abrupt end. Little did anyone realise that within two years the entire prison would be emptied ("decanted" to use the prison language) with the women and the staff scattered around the country, often very far from family living in and around London.

November 2015: announcement of the closure of HMP Holloway

On 25 November 2015, I saw a familiar colleague running in the direction of the chapel. She asked if I was coming, and I asked why. She said the closure of the prison is going to be announced. Therapy colleagues and I made our way to the chapel to hear that indeed the prison was closing and that a number of other Victorian jails would be sold in order to help fund nine new prisons. In a written statement the Justice Secretary Michael Gove said that Holloway's design and physical state did not provide the best environment for the rehabilitation of offenders (Prison Announcement, 2015).

As HMP Holloway was the only female prison in London, the closure of the MBU and later the entire prison presented serious problems for family members wishing to visit. Located in North London, HMP Holloway was accessible to London-based families. The prison was near two large train stations and had good public transport links for families to visit. Maintaining family ties is well recognised as a key influence in reducing re-offending. Moving prisoners far away from family is a serious issue and was a key topic in Baroness Corston's report (Corston, 2007) which was commissioned after the deaths in custody of six female prisoners at HMP Styal in one year. Comments about the report included journalists asserting that "we should no longer use the prison system as a dustbin for the disturbed. We are persecuting some of the most damaged and vulnerable women in society" (Guardian, 2008).

"De-canting" the therapeutic model

With the closing of HMP Holloway MBU, I was pleased that in 2007, I had already established the Born Inside project at a prison on the outskirts of London called HMP Bronzefield. The establishment of the project coincided with the publication of the Corston Report (Corston, 2007). I was able to begin the Born Inside project thanks to the vision and help of a very charismatic woman, Olga Heaven, and her excellent charity, Hibiscus, who support foreign nationals. Given the high percentage of foreign nationals on the MBUs, I had over the years made very strong connections with Hibiscus. Having good relationships with other services is vital to working in prisons. Forensic work demands a capacity to cooperate with and respect colleagues of other disciplines which included (but are not limited to) officers, probation staff, health visitors, doctors as well other therapists. Working with a wide range of staff is a corner stone of forensic psychotherapy. This work is all about building relationship and is what we learned at HMP Holloway. Focusing on clear, constructive relationships can be applied to other prisons. This was the key to the success of psychotherapy at Holloway. We hope to take this further to other prisons.

Working with colleagues

Further working and thinking together was supported by the setting up of clinical forums by our supervisor Dr Paola Franciosi. The forums provided a space where professionals could meet regularly to discuss their work and to consider different ways of thinking about our patients and the institution, as well as improving ways of working together. The forums acknowledged the importance of having a dedicated thinking space set aside. All who worked with and were inspired by Dr Franciosi carry this rich experience with us in our on-going work. Not only did Dr Franciosi encourage me to establish a weekly therapy group for pregnant women as well as the mothers on the MBU, she also encouraged reflective practice groups for the mental health teams. Being able to listen to and cooperate with other therapists, agencies and professionals is not only in the best interests of the prisoners but it is also essential for the mental health of the therapist – in conjunction with supervision. Beware the omnipotent therapist who works in isolation, eschewing supervision and reflective practice groups. Such therapists are damaging to their patients. Many of us were later supported by weekly supervision with Professor Gill McGauley whose untimely death in 2016 shocked and saddened us all.

Endings, looking back and moving on

So much has happened. So many years have passed. As I am writing my thoughts are with Luther and Gabrielle. Luther would be around twenty years old now and his mother, forty years old. I wonder if he is in prison. I have not come across Gabrielle. Many mothers do return to prison. Some mothers come and greet me. They say they are sorry they are back but remember the groups. One mother said, "For a little while I could be an ordinary mum and love my baby." As both of Luther's parents were imprisoned, the possibility that he and any siblings might spend time in prison are high. However, I have heard from many of the mothers over the years who tell me that they have not reoffended and are back working in the community leading orderly and ordinary lives. Worrying implications of imprisonment, such as the impact on children of their parents' imprisonment, can feel at times very distracting for a psychotherapist. However, keeping the social context in mind is also a serious consideration for psychotherapy as well as an important political issue.

The long-term impact on prisoner's children is a very important topic for consideration. US research indicates that having a parent incarcerated increases a child's chances of juvenile delinquency by 300–400 per cent; it increases the odds of serious psychiatric disorder by 250 per cent (Gladwell, 2013: 245). More resources should be allocated to understand the impact of parental imprisonment on children. Early interventions, such as the pregnancy and mother and baby groups are one way of highlighting the damaging impact on a child of having a mother in prison. With this in mind, instead of reducing the spaces of mother and baby units surely, they should be expanded? US research indicates lower re-offending rates for mothers who have kept their babies with them on mother and baby units (Robins, 2012).

What did I learn over all these years? For one thing I was wrong. The paradox of prison was not that it was a place of such great anxiety that a mother could not have a thoughtful relationship with her baby. As with Luther and Gabrielle, and so many others over the twenty years, the prison offered a safe environment where they were both physically and mentally contained, supported by a range of people who could see connections between their feelings and their subsequent actions. In time, many mothers made these links too. Hence, against my previous hypothesis, prison appeared to provide for many, a better opportunity to be a mother than was available in the community. Also, I learned that psychotherapy is not the province only for the worried well. Many of the most damaged and vulnerable women in our society did not experience the prison as a dustbin. As one mother said to me, "I never would have had this help if I had been at home." One of the developments from this is the creation of the Saturday Forensic Forum where clinical discussions continue to reaffirm our experience of how well many inmates use psychotherapy to develop insight and understanding about their offending and themselves. Insight is a great protector against the impulsive act. As one of my patients convicted of murder said to me:

> If I had had someone to talk to I never would have killed her. Even my children can see the difference in me now. They laugh and say hey, mum, now you ask about how we are feeling. Now you use more words when you talk with us.

We like to imagine that knowledge is power. Is it? Knowledge of injustice creates an ethical responsibility to do something once we know about injustice. Psychoanalysis places great emphasis on thinking while being very sceptical about action. Has this hindered the social importance of psychoanalytic insights? Is action always acting out? Against my early hypothesis I discovered that it is not prison that is the problem. Prison is a social symptom. All of us must share responsibility for the social elements that produces people who engage in criminal behaviours. The fact that we do not do this raises the question: why do we need prisons in the first place? With 69 per cent of prisoners reoffending within one year (Prison Reform Trust, 2017) can we say that prisons work in reducing offending and cutting down crime? Clear's (1996) research suggests that putting a large number of people in prison might have the opposite effect of reducing reoffending. What does this mean about our own need to have an underclass to deprive and then to punish?

As a result of the Born Inside project, I went on to train as a psychotherapist and have worked as a psychotherapist seeing individual female offenders as well as continuing the Born Inside groups. On good days at HMP Holloway, I felt that the prison psychotherapy service, supported by regular meetings and excellent supervision as well as clinical forums was a "surprising survivor of the therapeutic community model" (Taylor, 2014: 272). Working as a therapist in HMP Holloway kept me in touch with one of the most important realities for a forensic therapist. Don't work in isolation. Watch out for huge rises in anxiety which can compel the therapist to try and save the day. You need good colleagues for this. To work in a prison is to be able to "tolerate the bad object that cannot be repaired" (Bell, 2004: 21) in the hope of understanding the prison and my role in it. In the words of the philosopher Benedict de Spinoza, "I have striven not to laugh at human actions, to weep at them or to hate them, but to understand them" (Bell, 2004: viii).

Going back to the origins I am now more grateful than ever for the observational experience that prompted and has underpinned this work over twenty years. One of the most important things I learned to look out for is omnipotence; when to detect huge anxiety in myself and watch for trying to save the day. There are indeed times when you must walk away, awful as that is. I had learned to tolerate the bad object that could not be repaired. I will conclude with one of the early observations.

Martha (mother) drugs importation and Cinnamon (thirteen months)

On Monday I arrived as usual on the unit. The prison office came out of the glass walled office and suggested that instead of going to sit in my usual spot I first go into Martha's cell. The officer remarked in a very sad voice that Martha had been sentenced for drugs importation on Friday. "She's been sentenced to fourteen years – a tougher sentence than murder", the officer sighed. The officer's voice and the request expressed a sense of urgency to me. I sensed the officer wanted me to "do" something. She valued me or at least thought I had something to offer. I felt worried and confused.

The facts of going to trial are brutal whatever the outcome. The baby attends court with the mother. Once at court the baby is handed over to a court official and kept in the cells under the courtrooms. I imagine being in such a tense environment with many strange faces is disturbing for a baby. I was thinking about this and the very long sentence as I walked down the narrow corridor to Martha's cell. Prostrate on her narrow bed Martha's head was buried in her pillow. Barely looking up, Martha was able to catch my eye.

I asked her if she wanted me to go away. "No, stay", she said into the pillow. "I know Cinnamon will be taken from me. But she will be walkin' then, she will be talkin' then. She can run away from danger."

Afraid of being a voyeur in the presence of so much grief and wishing I could escape I again asked if she wanted me to go. Again, she said no. We sat in silence for twenty minutes as she lay with her head buried in her own arms. I resisted the impulse to hold her.

The cell was a mess – clothes everywhere. Drawers half opened. By the sink was a full baby bottle of milk. Martha looked up at me looking at the bottle. She said "Cinnamon, she jus' like me, she feels jus' like me; she ain't eatin'."

Martha said she had slept for the first time in months last night. Sleep had been impossible on Friday and Saturday. Martha said that she kept thinking about her seven other children back in the Caribbean.

"Will they be thieves and prostitutes without me?" She wailed and tossed her head, rubbing her eyes. Finally, she yawned and stretched, flexing and pointing her feet. She sighed, saying she was sleepy now. I said in that case I will go now. Nodding, she looked nearly asleep.

On my way to the large room where I held the mother and baby group I could see that it looked empty. No one had come to the group that day. As I got closer there was one tiny exception. Cinnamon sat alone in the large room. How did she get there? Had Martha left her for me? Looking dishevelled and uncombed she was tearing furiously at a teat she had pulled from a full, now spilled, bottle of milk. She looked into the empty space with an expression of dizzy despair. I had to accept that I could do nothing apart from informing the officer that the baby was alone in the nursery.

Having waited nearly a year for her trial Martha was given a huge sentence, a sentence so long that even the officer was shocked. In the face of this everyone had lost sight of Cinnamon. No one could hold on to her and what her mother's sentence would mean for her and her siblings. Although Martha could identify with her daughter's inability to eat she was incapable of finding room in her own mind to think about her child.

It felt as if Martha had to distance herself from her daughter's distress so flooded did she feel by her own. Not even the bottle could contain the milk. Nothing felt firm or solid. I had to accept there was nothing I could do apart from witness and later reflect on the damage and despair. Leaving the prison, the natural light hurt my eyes. In the MBU, it felt as if it had been the middle of a very wintry, dark day. In fact, the sun was shining and the air in North London was breezy and fresh.

2018: not the end of the sentence

The Mother and Baby Born Inside project is currently on-going at HMP Bronzefield where individual psychotherapy and many therapy groups are also provided by the Mental Health In-reach team. Other therapeutic interventions, such as Jess Collier's work as an art therapist, are also available at HMP Downview. Reflective practice groups take place at both prisons and much that of what was learned by colleagues from Holloway is evolving in these two prisons. The closing of HMP Holloway has not meant an end to the work begun there.

ACKNOWLEDGEMENTS

The Born Inside groups at HMP Bronzefield are currently funded by the International Montessori Institute (MMI), which is an affiliation to the Association Montessori Internationale (AMI). The groups are co-facilitated by Beverley Maragh, lecturer and antenatal teacher.

REFERENCES

Barnado's (2017). Mother and Baby Prison Units: An investigative study. Available at: www.barnardos.org.uk/what_we_do/our_work/children_of_prisoners.htm. Date accessed: 1 February 2018.

Bell, D. (2004). *Reason and passion: A celebration of the work of Hanna Segal.* London: Karnac Books.

Bick, E. (1964). Infant observation in psychoanalytic training. *International Journal of Psycho-Analysis*, 45: 558–566.

Clear, T. (1996). Backfire: When incarceration increased crime. In: T. Gash (ed.), *Why people do bad things* (p.14). London: Penguin.2016.

Corston, J. (2007). *The Corston Report: A review of women with particular vulnerabilities in the criminal justice system.* London: Home Office.

Didion, J (1963). *Run River.* University of Michigan: Pocket Books.

Douglas, N., Plugge, E. and Fitzpatrick, R. (2009). The impact of imprisonment on health: What do women prisoners say? *Journal of Epidemiology & Community Health*, 63: 749–754.

Fazel, S., Hayes, A., Bartellas, K., Clerici, M. and Trestman, R. (2016). Mental health of prisoners: Prevalence, adverse outcomes, and interventions. *The Lancet Psychiatry*, 3: 871–881.

Foster, H. (2012). The strains of maternal imprisonment: Importation and deprivation stressors for women and children. *Journal of Criminal Justice*, 40: 221–229.

Foucault, M. (1977). *Discipline and punish: The birth of the prison.* New York: Vintage Books.

Gladwell, M. (2013). *David and Goliath: Underdogs, misfits, and the art of battling giants.* London: Penguin.

Guardian. (2008). A shameful way to treat women prisoners. *The Guardian*, 30 March. Available at: www.theguardian.com/commentisfree/2008/mar/30/prisonsandprobation.gender. Date accessed: 30 July 2017.

Independent. (2017). Nearly half of female prisoners have attempted suicide, figures reveal. Available at: www.independent.co.uk/news/uk/home-news/female-prisoners-suicide-death-rate-mental-health-nearly-half-attempt-figures-reveal-prison-reform-a7724171.html. Date accessed: 13 February 2018.

MacDonald, M. (2013). Women prisoners, mental health, violence and abuse. *International Journal of Law and Psychiatry*, 36: 293–303.

Murray, J. (2005). The effects of imprisonment on families and children of prisoners. In: A. Liebling and S. Maruna (eds), *The effects of imprisonment* (pp.442–492). England: Willan.

Prison Announcement. (2015). Written Ministerial Statement made by the Lord Chancellor and Secretary of State for Justice, Michael Gove. 25 November. Available at: www.gov.uk/government/speeches/prisons-announcement. Date accessed: 11 December 2017.

Prison Reform Trust. (2015). Why focus on reducing women's imprisonment? A prison reform trust briefing [Online]. Available at: www.prisonreformtrust.org.uk/Portals/0/Documents/Women/why women.pdf. Date accessed: 15 January 2018.

Prison Reform Trust. (2017). Prison: The facts. Bromley Briefings. Available at: www.prisonreformtrust.org.uk/Portals/0/Documents/Bromley%20Briefings/Autumn%202017%20factfile.pdf. Date accessed: 27 January 2018.

Reed, S. (1997). *Developments in Infant Observation: The Tavistock Model*. London: Routledge.

Robins, L. (2012). Mother and baby prison units: An investigative study. Available at: www.communitymatters.govt.nz/vwluResources/WCMT_Libby_Robins_2011_Final/$file/WCMT_Libby_Robins_2011_Final.pdf. Date accessed: 4 March 2018.

Strout, E. (2016). *My name is Lucy Barton*. London: Penguin.

Taylor, B. (2014). *The asylum: A memoir of madness in our times*. London: Hamish Hamilton.

Welldon, E. (2000). *Mother, Madonna, whore: The idealisation and denigration of motherhood*. London: Karnac Books.

CHAPTER THREE

Who's holding the baby?

Containment, dramatherapy and the pregnant therapist

Lorna Downing and Lorraine Grout

Introduction

Dramatherapy is inconceivable without acknowledging the body. Dramatherapists use their own bodies in therapy sessions to model and mirror their patients, actively encouraging immersion in the creative process. This can be particularly poignant when working with female patients who may have complex relationships with their own bodies and who frequently "act out" violently against themselves, others and their environment. The pregnant therapist and her ever-changing body adds another important dimension to working within the confinement of the metaphorical brick mother.

At HMP Holloway, the health care unit day centre offered arts activities and therapies for female forensic patients with mental health difficulties. It held a conflicted position of care and punishment within the prison regime. "Acting out" while confined on the unit might often lead to further punishment including loss of privileges or increased medication. This potentially left patients silenced and in a stuck state of hopelessness and inertia. The aim of using dramatherapy in this setting was to support patients to access their hidden internal worlds and encourage "a safe way to allow the unspeakable to be spoken" (Downing in Rothwell, 2016: 250).

Renée Emunah suggests that "When acting out is translated into acting, the result is often a powerful form of communication and therapy" (Emunah, 1995: 154). Work with the body and "acting" of any kind, can be met with resistance in a prison, often bringing with it the fear that unmanageable behaviours might be provoked and amplified. The dramatherapist is tasked with demonstrating she is capable of maintaining the boundaries firmly and safely while simultaneously protecting the therapeutic "holding environment" (Winnicott, 1965: 47). Welldon (2004) and Motz (2008, 2009) have highlighted the capacity of women to commit violent and perverse crimes. Yet within this setting, there remained a tendency to associate the women with the role of victim; perhaps as a more acceptable and less frightening version of the "feminine".

Nevertheless, the arrival of a pregnant dramatherapist into an "essentially masculine (environment)", (Ramsbotham in Saunders, 2001: xv) unwittingly communicates her innate femaleness; inciting new projections from staff and patients. On this unit, already overwhelmed with intense projections and perpetually facing the likelihood of physical and psychic attack, the institution may have perceived pregnancy as an additional risk. Patients may have considered the pregnant therapist to be too fragile or too full to hold their negative emotions. In this situation, the unborn child becomes an unwanted imposter, a third person in the relationship, who will ultimately steal the therapist away. "There are initially only two players in this dance and drama of life" (Jennings, 2011: 20).

In ordinary life, pregnancy and the birth of a baby usually comes with a sense of hope. However, incarcerated women, separated from their own families, may experience this differently. A pregnancy within the therapeutic relationship may elicit intense, unresolved feelings regarding the absence of the woman's own baby or dreams of motherhood. There may be envy around the fantasy of the fresh start a baby brings. The patients may view pregnancy as an opportunity to recreate a better, unspoiled version of themselves and a chance to right the wrongs, through creating what Anna Motz describes as "a narcissistic extension of themselves ... The baby can be seen as the good object which the 'bad' women desperately needs as a receptacle for her projection" (Motz, 2008: 10).

The pregnant therapist who knowingly takes her unborn child into a volatile and psychologically precarious environment could also be considered a "bad mother". Her presence may potentially bring the unspoken concept of perverse mothering into the therapeutic space. While the tension between motherhood and professional life is a common dilemma for working mothers, working in a forensic environment can invite additional criticism and projections that may become exaggerated by the risk and disturbance that is ever present. Pregnancy muddies traditional clinical boundaries and the neutral stance of the therapist is inevitably compromised. Visible disclosure that the therapist has a life outside the prison which must include intimate and sexual relationships can expose her to new projections and identifications. On seeing Lorna's pregnant belly, one patient laughed and yelled, "You're a dirty bitch just like the rest of us." This might be seen as an attempt at closeness, and pregnancy can offer a new opening in the therapeutic relationship. However, careful consideration of the changes in the transference is required in order to reduce risk and protect the patient, pregnant therapist and the unborn child.

This chapter is a retrospective snapshot of the work of two dramatherapists, Lorna Downing and Lorraine Grout, during their pregnancies at two different stages in the life cycle of HMP Holloway. We will use case material and discussion to think about the complexities and contrast of the living, flesh mother within the static brick mother, and what pregnancy evokes in the therapist, patient and institution. This offers a unique opportunity to explore the question: "Who's holding the baby?"

Background

Lorna and Lorraine worked as dramatherapists on the health care unit thirteen years apart: Lorna from 1999 to 2004 and Lorraine from 2014 to 2015. Despite this sizable interval, the presentation of the patients remained similar. Paralleling the rest of the prison, the patients were a mix of diverse ages, backgrounds, cultures, index offences and diagnoses. However, health care patients were usually admitted to the unit for close monitoring because they had exhibited overt psychotic symptoms, suicidal ideation or a particular vulnerability that might need additional care, protection and assessment. This meant that they were further excluded, not only from society, but denigrated by the main prison population too. The transient nature of the patients meant developing a sustained therapeutic relationship was difficult. Self-harming was prolific and aims of rehabilitation were not always achieved, due in part to strains on resources and staffing. The health care unit was under constant pressure to prevent successful suicide attempts. It was challenging and often regarded with fear and disdain by the rest of the prison. This confined environment existed as "a container-within-the-container", mirroring the pregnant dramatherapist and the boundaries of the therapeutic relationship. Holding both her patients fragmented sense of self and her developing baby, the therapist could sometimes feel in "two minds" herself.

When Lorna was working at HMP Holloway in 2001, the health care unit was managed not by the NHS, but by the prison service. Hard-working prison staff were inadequately trained to deal with the acute levels of disturbance. Therapy, sometimes regarded with suspicion, was often perceived as superfluous and "pointless" for female offenders with this level of psychological disturbance. By 2014, when Lorraine began her trainee dramatherapy placement, the NHS had taken control. There was a multi-disciplinary team, ward rounds and development of clinical thinking was encouraged. However, there was no dramatherapist in post. Often patients on the health care unit were not offered talking therapy from the psychological therapies team. Resources were limited and clinical discussion often concluded that the women were not ready to engage in verbal psychotherapy, either because they were "pre pre-therapy" (Rothwell and Grandison, 2016: 185) or because they were due to move to hospital, be sentenced or transferred to another prison. The intervention of dramatherapy was the only group therapy available on the health care unit. However, by 2014, in addition to the group work, Lorraine was also able to take individual referrals from the psychological therapies team. This enabled more stable women residing on ordinary location within the main prison population to access dramatherapy.

The following vignettes are taken from dramatherapy sessions when Lorna and Lorraine were both pregnant. They explore four moments within dramatherapy sessions; the first two from Lorna's sessions and the second two from Lorraine's. All names of patients have been changed to protect confidentiality.

Finding a safe space

I began working at HMP Holloway in 1999, having qualified as a dramatherapist the year before. I facilitated seven weekly dramatherapy groups with a male co-facilitator. Often perceived as the dramatherapy "husband and wife", we were metaphorically holding many "babies". The sessions were well attended by regular patients and new admissions were occasionally brought in as part of their health care assessment. Often there would be no prior knowledge of a patient's history and no detailed handover. In these cases, unresolved feelings often emerged and the women's undisclosed offences might be "played out" in the dramatic process. It was vital that both facilitators were vigilant in containing these aspects safely and sensitive to transferential material. They would attempt to process this together pre and post session.

Bringing in the baby

At the time of the following vignette, the health care unit was in "survival mode". Reeling from a combination of high profile cases, an inquest, two suicides, and the dismissal of the only medically qualified consultant psychiatrist, the unit felt traumatised and unsafe. This left limited space for clinical thinking.

I was in the first trimester of my second pregnancy and struggling with morning sickness. My conflicting responsibilities as mother and dramatherapist made me hesitant about entering an unsettled environment. Unfamiliar feelings of ambivalence at work were tempered with overwhelming bouts of sadness and unexpected surges of rage. I felt a sense of injustice heightened by recent deaths on the unit. My co-facilitator was the only staff member who knew I was pregnant. I shared with him that I was feeling "all over the place" and we both noted that I could be somatically experiencing the unit's trauma. On this occasion and with this trauma in mind we started a session; "creating a safe space". We began with some mindful movement, stretching and breathing, to gently warm up the body and create a potential space for active imagination. The five regular attendees, well versed in the dramatherapy group rituals, indirectly assisted. Using a dramatherapy technique known as "sculpting", each person created their version of a "safe space"; in this instance using other group members to create a scene. For the purpose of this vignette, I will focus on a new member of the group that day, whom I will call Kelly.

Kelly was a pale, anxious-looking woman in her twenties. When she first arrived she seemed unsure what was expected of her. Following the others lead, she tentatively positioned the group members as; a single bed, a chest of drawers, a cupboard. Despite the large space available Kelly had created a small, stark bedroom. My immediate thoughts were that it closely resembled a prison cell. I wondered if Kelly was illustrating that prison is where she feels safe. Another group member shouted, "What no ligature points?" The rest of the group laughed at this sinister reference to the prison's attempts to restrict suicide opportunities. Kelly added a window and then a door. She demonstrated opening and closing this, before closing it firmly, stating it was now locked. When offered the option to share her "safe space" with someone, Kelly introduced her seven month old baby daughter to the scene using a bunched up piece of cloth which she placed on the bed. Kelly also added her dog "for protection". She said he was a pit bull terrier, "who would stop any peters [thieves] getting in". When invited to position *herself* within her "safe space" Kelly did not choose to sit with her baby but stood staring blankly out the "window". The "safe space" was compromised by the vulnerable infant who, unsupported at seven months, might at any moment fall off the bed. The baby was also in close proximity to a fierce dog. The imagined scene presented a tableau of victim and perpetrator cohabiting. Kelly stood in the centre, apparently turning a blind eye to this dangerous scene, possibly unable to make the connection. Kelly seemed to be illustrating her own feelings of ambivalence towards her infant. Ignoring the potential risks, she had demonstrated her inability to respond to her baby's needs. Perhaps Kelly's own mother had not been able to keep her safe. The danger seemed screamingly obvious, but nothing was said.

As dramatherapists we are continually working with countertransference. During this session I experienced a sudden overwhelming sense of unease. In utero, my developing baby quickened for the first time, flipping over, I imagined, as if "falling off a bed". I stepped back, automatically placing my hand on my belly and felt horribly conscious that I too had brought a baby into an unsafe space. Immediately I felt exposed and vulnerable. On witnessing this, a group member asked, "Are you pregnant, Miss?" I responded by pretending I hadn't heard, desperate to keep my pregnancy concealed. My immediate urge, perhaps responding to my own baby, was to rescue Kelly's "baby" and bring her to safety. I wanted to escape the "bad mothers" and run away home. Prior to my pregnancy I had sometimes struggled with feeling that I over identified with patients. Now I unexpectedly desired separateness and safety. My fear of contagion felt very real and I wanted to get away. Anna Motz, describing her own experience as a pregnant therapist and the change on the transference relationship, says; "perhaps it is only at times of great vulnerability in the therapist that . . . memories and thoughts become vivid and appear in the transference as immediate threats to psychic or physical safety"

(Motz, 2008: 62). I felt overwhelmed with projections and my response left me too "full" to process these. It was not until much later that I began to consider that, in my "porous" pregnant state, I may have been vicariously holding the unspoken trauma experienced first-hand by the patients.

"The Red Shoes": shame, scars and surviving the uncontainable

At seven months, my large pregnant belly was impossible to conceal, particularly when accentuated by the ever-tightening mandatory prison key belt. In private, I took comfort in sharing stories, songs and comments on the world with my baby. However, in public I experienced a sense that I had lost my identity and become a member of a faceless "baby container" community. Patients and staff would touch my bump without asking. Everyone asked me unsolicited questions about "the baby". Working in HMP Holloway, I feared being judged or being forced to join an antenatal club where I felt I didn't belong. Simultaneously, the unit felt more settled; as if the recent suicides had been forgotten and everything had returned to normal.

Stories have a containing function. Working with archetypes and metaphor can unearth hidden truths. These help to make sense of the world and rework traumatic experiences. The lesser-known Magyar-Germanic version of "The Red Shoes" was used in the following vignette. The story focuses on the protagonist's quest to find a replacement for the lost handmade red rag shoes she has treasured as a child. The runaway substitute "shoes", mirrored a dance towards destruction and the patient's life spiralling out of control through the experience of addiction and psychosis, which was too painful to speak about meaningfully.

Following an episode of self-harm, during which she had used a broken dance music CD to lacerate her arms, Julie, a talkative, twenty year old woman, had been transferred to the health care unit. She told the group she had a mixed diagnosis of borderline personality disorder and, giggling, described an episode of drug-induced psychosis. Julie spoke freely about her index offence of "clipping"; luring a potential "punter" for sex with the intention of robbing him. As she spoke there was a sense we were not hearing the full story. Julie minimised her suffering and shame. She joked about being out of control and "off her head".

On this day my co-facilitator was on leave and four women attended the dramatherapy session. This female group had a different feel to it and perhaps prompted by my pregnancy, allowed a space for women to speak more freely about their monthly cycles. The "red", in fairy tales is often a metaphor for blood; the onset of menstruation and transition into adulthood. Julie mentioned her periods restarting having come off heroin. She described how she had cried the night before and felt her "emotions flooding back". Julie recalled a boy at school taking a sanitary towel out of her bag and "shaming" her in front of everyone on the bus. I wondered about the collective shame of women regarding this natural bodily function and the expectation to conceal rather than celebrate the onset.

In the enactment of the story, Julie volunteered to take on the main role; a motherless child living in the forest in her handmade red rag shoes. On the road, she meets a rich old lady in a gilded carriage who invites her to live in her mansion, but in return she loses her freedom. Trapped and forced to conform, her naturally wild nature is stifled and her precious rag shoes burnt. Bereft of her original handmade shoes, Julie, in role, becomes obsessed with her desire for the new scandalous red shoes, glowing "like burnished apples". She spies them in the shoemakers and sneaks them past the short-sighted old lady. She brazenly wears them to church and is met with a chorus of disapproving whisperers, scorning and excluding her. All except for an injured soldier, who winks, and asks if she is staying for the dance. Julie's feet then began to move "of their own accord". Starting tentatively to the slow beat of a drum, her breadth of movement got faster until it became a frantic gesture, her blonde hair swaying. The rest of the group began stomping their feet and clapping rhythmically to a climax, broken only by exhausted Julie begging the executioner to "Cut them off!"

There was silence as the group caught their breath. Julie sighed and crumpled in her seat. A moment later there was a sudden screech of chair legs as another, usually disinterested, group member got to her feet and walked purposely towards Julie. Picking up a piece of costume cloth, she sat down heavily next to Julie, reached down and began to gently "bandage" her feet. This powerful moment seemed to bring the unspoken rituals of self-harm and after care into the therapy room, allowing it to be witnessed. There was another pause. Julie indicated she was ok, but the moment was brutally interrupted by the introduction of an improvised happy ending by another group member. A new character, "The Prince", appeared and offered his hand in marriage.

Julie smiled and slumped back in her chair, put her bandaged "feet" up and yelled at the "Prince", "Cuppa tea love. Two sugars!" The bathos of the "cuppa tea" moment prompted laughter from the group, perhaps as a defence, discharging anxiety but also normalising the violence. The group seemed unable to hold onto the cutting and I wondered whether they unconsciously feared that the pregnant therapist and unborn child would be damaged by the brutal truth.

Having de-roled the characters, there was an opportunity for reflection, and Julie spoke of the exhilaration and belonging she had experienced in her teens, taking ecstasy and being part of the clubbing culture. She recounted how this came to an abrupt end when she witnessed her best friend's seizure, convulsing in time with the beeps of the life support machine, unable to stop "dancing". Julie described her descent into addiction in an attempt to fill the void and the feeling of being shunned and "dis-membered" by society (Adlam and Scanlon, 2009: 131). By immersing herself in her fictional role, Julie was able to re-enact aspects of her own experience through projection and rework some of her life's trauma from an aesthetic distance. There was a fresh authenticity in her narrative in which she detailed false promises, shame, deception and loss. "The Red Shoes" seemed to have a transformative and healing effect. Despite the inability of the group to stay with the pain, the invention of a happy ending offered Julie, the group, the pregnant therapist and the baby, respite from real life traumas. Alongside this transformational quality the group's action temporarily alleviated my guilt at leaving my Holloway "babies".

Julie spoke with positivity regarding plans for her future and the women shared tales of survival. Having previously "lost their footing" there was an awareness of the dangers of falling in to another trap in the future. I wondered about being temporarily "dis-membered" from the group while I was on maternity leave, and potentially putting my therapist's feet up.

The mirror

As a trainee on placement I had a confirmed finish date established with my patients from the beginning of our work together. My maternity due date came after this. I worked on the health care unit at HMP Holloway for nine months facilitating an open dramatherapy group with the intention of including as many women as possible. The following vignette is from a session when I was two months pregnant with my first child. Although not visibly pregnant, I was feeling quite "full" with university work, my job and my developing baby. At times I felt under pressure and my thinking itself often felt pressured. Just before starting my placement at HMP Holloway there had been a death in custody. There was therefore, a feeling that everyone was on high alert.

Initially, having discovered I was pregnant, I felt well. Nevertheless, I became concerned about my key belt and where it sat on my body each time I put it on. I was intensely aware of my belly growing. At this time I had not told any staff of my pregnancy as I had not yet had my twelve week scan and was nervous. I didn't want to ask for help but was struggling to unload and pack up my dramatherapy equipment alone. During this time, I noticed a patient sitting quietly, following me with her eyes as I moved around the unit. This felt unsettling and highlighted my "great vulnerability" as a pregnant therapist (Motz, 2008: 62).

Nicola was known to be unpredictable and violent. Three officers were required to be present when she came out of her cell. As she became more settled, Nicola expressed a curiosity in what was happening in the dramatherapy group. On her first visit, she had struggled to be in a group with others and had left. However, a few weeks later, she came to the session and was the only patient present.

Immediately, Nicola picked up a large cushioned ball. I held out my hands for her to instigate play and the beginnings of a "dialogue", but she did not respond. I picked up another ball and began mirroring her movements from the other side of the therapy room. Nicola smiled, keeping eye contact and playfully seeing if I would follow all her movements. This silent exchange between us continued for fifteen minutes and she seemed to be enjoying me reflecting back her movements. The action then shifted to something more sexualised as Nicola mimed penetrating the ball. She began asking me personal questions, laughing as she did so. In this moment she seemed nervous. I wondered if Nicola was testing the therapist's boundaries in an attempt to make a connection in the only way she knew how; through sex. Once she had established that I could hold this boundary and my intent was to attempt to keep her safe, the energy changed. We sat down and the mirroring continued in a sitting position. Nicola began to describe being sexually abused as a child and young person. She added that her violent index offence had been against a female clinician and that she had been given a diagnosis of post-partum psychosis. Nicola asked in a humorous, affronted way, "Do you think I'm going to attack you?"

I could see vulnerability in her threatening question, but I was also acutely aware of the potential risk I was in.

As we continued, the ball came to represent different things to Nicola; her comfort, her own child and her anger. She seemed to want to offload all her bad experiences and I had the sense she had told these painful tales before. I invited her to join me in a further dramatherapy technique and we moved on to mirroring verbally. By repeating her sentences back to her as she said them, she could witness herself and her pain. This enabled her to answer her own questions. After describing a sexual attack where she was the victim, she said "I'm a slag. Wish I could erase that part of my life. Do you think that was wrong?" Nicola finished the session by acknowledging the ball had been with her throughout. I asked her what she wanted to leave behind and what she might take with her. Nicola chose to leave behind her pain, hurt, guilt, shame and disgust. She said she would take with her joy and happiness and the excitement of being with her son. When I asked her to leave the ball behind and cross back over the dramatherapy threshold Nicola acknowledged the ball had held her emotions. I believe for this woman, the mirroring gave her a feeling of safety, control and intimate sharing where "the usual boundaries between people dissolve" (Emunah, 1995: 151). It allowed her to access these traumatic events in a new safe way where perhaps closeness had been previously associated with abuse. She seemed able to trust the dramatherapy process and the roles I held for her. This was Nicola's first and last session; she was released the next day. I thought about the moment when we had sat mirroring each other, the ball on our laps, and how Nicola had referenced herself as a child while I had the knowledge that my own child was in the room too. It seemed as if the full developmental phase of embodiment, protection and role had been achieved in this one dramatherapy session (Jennings, 2011: 15).

Too close for comfort: no safe place

In October 2014, I was referred my first individual dramatherapy patient through the psychological therapies clinical meeting.

Lisa resided in ordinary location, the main part of the prison. She had a history of violent offending towards women and was serving three years for actual bodily harm (ABH) against a random stranger. Lisa had mobility issues and struggled either to move or to be still. Despite this, in the nineteen weeks we worked together, she transferred cell eight times. Each time I was tasked with finding her in the prison to continue our work, recreating her personal experiences of unsafe home environments, homelessness and the ambivalent relationship with her mother. Lisa often described her mother looking for her when she went missing. It seemed this feeling of being rescued was something Lisa was compelled to re-enact repeatedly.

When I first met Lisa I was not pregnant. Her cell door hatch was open and I knocked. I was immediately aware of her intimidating stature and aggressive stance. She looked up and demanded "Are you the nurse?" I replied "No, I'm Lorraine the dramatherapist". Lisa's expression changed. She smiled warmly and leant her arm through the hatch to greet me. I felt a wave of fear as though she had the capacity to twist my arm and drag me through the hatch and in to her cell. I never forgot this first interaction and her ability to switch roles between victim and perpetrator depending on her needs. This moment seemed to encapsulate Lisa's difficulty with relationships and her inability to feel safely contained. She seemed to set up a "painful oscillation" (Motz, 2009: 68), "where intimacy is perceived as annihilating and separateness is perceived as an abandoned state" (Glasser in Holloway, Seebohm and Dokter, 2011: 127).

At this point I was still less than three months pregnant and had two months left at my placement. I was in the process of developing two new roles; as a mother and qualified therapist. I noticed that I had begun to check in with my baby at the prison gate. I felt anxious about needing to go to the toilet or feeling nauseous while with a patient. I was conflicted that no one knew I was pregnant and it being too early to make the announcement. I was also finding it harder to focus and I needed extra time to ground myself in preparation for sessions. As I got closer to my twelve week scan I noticed my belly was becoming harder.

During our thirteenth session, Lisa described some details of her offences. "I don't know why I slapped a women down the street. I don't think I was very well, and I barged into an old lady." Lisa looked angry when she spoke about the old lady. I asked her what was on her mind. "The man who broke my jaw when I was fifteen didn't get prosecuted!" I felt as though Lisa wanted me to feel her anger, injustice and the pain that no one had protected her. She then spoke about when she was homeless and walking down Oxford Street and how overwhelming that had felt. Although apprehensive, Lisa accepted my invitation to move through a therapeutic enactment. I gently invited her to cross a threshold in to the dramatic space, acknowledging the transition of stepping in and out of role for safety. We were both aware that we were working directly with the circumstances leading up to her index offence. Lisa instructed me what to do and created the following scene. She asked me to walk towards her as a member of the public and gently bump in to her. I asked what would happen next.

LISA: "The first person, I will say 'sorry' because that's what you do."
LORRAINE: "Okay, what about the next person?"
> We began to walk together and repeated the movement. Each time after the moment of contact Lisa moved out of the scene and leant against the wall.

LISA: "The next person, I will start to get annoyed, as it hurts my back when people bump into me."
LORRAINE: "Okay, what happens next?"
LISA: "I will find somewhere to rest, probably a bus stop, because my back's sore and I need to rest, one pain triggering another."
> Lisa sat down on a chair. Sensing she was finding this difficult I asked her to come out of the scene and work projectively, substituting chairs for people. Now that both of us were looking from the outside at the scene we continued;

LORRAINE: "What happens then?"
LISA: "People start asking me questions, 'excuse me do you know ...'"
LORRAINE: "What do you say?"
LISA: "Oh fuck off!"

I asked Lisa to notice how she was feeling at this point, to de-role and cross back over the threshold. I then suggested she write down her feelings starting with "I feel ..." and read them out aloud. Lisa ended the session saying "I think my family rely on me too much."

This was the first indication of a physical and mental shift in Lisa and seemed to reveal the part of her that was vulnerable to offending. The session allowed us both to witness where in Lisa's life she had merged moments of violence towards others with times when she herself had been assaulted. The injustice of one seamlessly assimilating into another, the concept of the victim and perpetrator, were firmly combined; mirroring her own experience of care. I wondered where Lisa felt safe, and if she was aware of her actions illustrating an unconscious longing to be contained.

Shortly after this session Lisa moved cells yet again. Her health deteriorated and three sessions later she terminated the therapeutic contract. I don't believe Lisa consciously knew I was pregnant. It was never noted and I was only in my first trimester. Unconsciously however, perhaps I had begun to represent her own mother and sibling who she would have to take care of again; the inevitable threat of change and also the vulnerable container. I also wondered if Lisa was trying to regress back to a safe place of being in utero; by creating a pseudo environment of holding and containment represented by the prison. If Lisa knew unconsciously that my uterus was no longer available, she would feel there was no space for her and see that it was time to move on. Having witnessed and tolerated both the perpetrator and the victim within her, perhaps Lisa expected me to disappear; replicating previous failed attempts at relationships. Rejecting me before I abandoned her allowed her to maintain a sense of control. I hope that our work together created foundations for a further therapeutic relationship.

Conclusion

> The circle of containment is established pre-birth as the infant is contained within the womb.
> (Jennings, 2011: 14)

Through this chapter, we hope to have offered a reflection on the complexities of working while pregnant with a variety of dramatherapy methods, with challenging patients in HMP Holloway. Exposure to the raw projections of the mother in a volatile environment where mothering is either idealised or perverse, offered a unique opportunity to explore the changes in the therapeutic relationship that are stimulated by pregnancy. Through their pregnancies Lorna and Lorraine encountered layered themes of connection between therapist and patient, mother and child and victim and perpetrator that highlight the tension between nurturing and punishment inherent in the prison environment.

Many dramatherapists have come through the gates of HMP Holloway over the years. Lorna returned post pregnancy and worked for a further three years before moving on. Lorraine successfully qualified and had intended to continue her work with the women. These plans were curtailed by the unexpected closure of the prison at a time when it was developing an exceptionally diverse psychological therapies team. This service attempted to provide opportunities for the women who were confined to think about the trans-generational patterns of abuse, neglect and violence that inevitably led to their offences.

Just as the feet in "The Red Shoes" are brutally cut, so HMP Holloway came to an abrupt end. We were left wondering "Who's holding the baby now?"

> I stand in the ring
> In the dead city
> And tie on the red shoes...
> They are not mine
> They are my mother's
> Her mother's before.
> Handed down like an heirloom
> But hidden like shameful letters.
> The house and the street where they
> Belong
> Are hidden and all the women, too
> Are hidden
>
> Sexton (1972: 28)

REFERENCES

Adlam, J and Scanlon, C (2009) Disturbances of "groupishness"? Structural violence, refusal and the therapeutic community response to severe personality disorder. *International Forum of Psychoanalysis* 18(1), 23–29.

Emunah, R (1995) From adolescent trauma to adolescent drama: group drama therapy with emotionally disturbed youth. In S. Jennings (eds), *Dramatherapy with Children and Adolescents*, 150–168. New York: Routledge.

Holloway, P, Seebohm, H, Dokter, D (eds) (2011) *Dramatherapy and Destructiveness: Creating the Evidence Base, Playing with Thanatos*. East Sussex: Routledge.

Jennings, S (2011) *Healthy Attachments and Neuro-Dramatic Play*. London: Jessica Kingsley.

Motz, A (2008) *The Psychology of Female Violence: Crimes against the Body*. London: Routledge.

Motz, A (2009) *Managing Self Harm: Psychological Perspectives*. Hove: Routledge.

Rothwell, K (2016) *Forensic Arts Therapies: Anthology of Practice and Research*. London: Free Association Books.

Rothwell, K, Grandison, R (2016) Notes on service design for art psychotherapists working in time-limited group programmes on adult mental health inpatient wards. In R Hughes (ed), *Time-Limited Art Psychotherapy: Developments in Theory and Practice*, 180–194. Abingdon: Routledge.

Saunders, J (2001) *Life within Hidden Worlds: Psychotherapy in Prisons*. London: Karnac.

Sexton, A (1972) *The Book of Folly*. London: Houghton Mifflin.

Welldon, E (2004) *Mother, Madonna, Whore: The Idealization and Denigration of Motherhood*. London: Karnac.

Winnicott, D W (1965) *The Maturational Processes and Facilitating Environment*. London: Hogarth Press.

PART II

WORKING WITH INSTITUTIONAL DYNAMICS

CHAPTER FOUR

Encountering HMP Holloway

A conversation

Paola Franciosi and Karen Rowe

Dr Paola Franciosi created and led the psychotherapy service at HMP Holloway for twenty-five years. In this chapter she and Karen Rowe, one of her former trainees, discuss the origins of the service, the difficulties she encountered and reflect on what she learned about forensic practice and the future of work with female offenders.

KR: *Why did you originally go to HMP Holloway and what were the circumstances of your appointment?*
PF: I had completed my training in psychotherapy and psychoanalytic psychotherapy and in 1990 I responded to an advertisement in the *British Medical Journal* for a part-time position as visiting consultant psychiatrist in psychotherapy at HMP Holloway. I arrived for a visit to the prison and introduced myself to the consultant whose job I was going to apply for. He did not know that his job had been advertised and it appeared that he had no intention of leaving his position. He said he must have been sacked without even being informed of his dismissal. From this moment I had the impression of how some things worked in this prison. There was no respect for anyone, prisoner or staff.

I did not have direct experience of a forensic psychotherapy setting when I took up my position at HMP Holloway. However, I had had the experience of undertaking psychoanalytic psychotherapy with women who had a history of emotional deprivation, physical and sexual abuse, separation from their parents, neglect and a forensic history. I felt that my experience in day based therapeutic communities was going to be very useful to me in the forensic context. There was a difference though; the women in prison not only had committed a crime, for which they were in custody, but were in a setting very different from a therapeutic community. They, and I, were in a place which I knew from the very beginning would be difficult and not conducive to a therapeutic approach.

KR: *When you arrived at HMP Holloway was there anything in place to support the women's mental health?*

PF: Initially I made contact with the visiting consultant psychiatrists. Their main commitment in the prison was writing reports for the courts and prescribing medication for patients if needed. They started referring patients to me for further assessment and for psychotherapeutic treatment if appropriate.

I made contact with the head of the psychology department and with the psychologists working there. They were forensic psychologists, which means that they were doing risk assessment and management of risk rather than any therapeutic intervention. At some point in the 1990s it began to feel as if the idea of providing psychological therapy for the women had entered the thinking and the vocabulary of the prison. A while later counselling psychologists were introduced and we worked very closely together for all the years I remained at HMP Holloway.

These colleagues, especially Barbara Beard, who was head of counselling psychology, were very supportive of the psychotherapy work. She had a clear position in the prison hierarchy and was, therefore able to effectively support us and raise our status within the organisation.

When I first started there were also two art psychotherapists, volunteering in the education unit, with whom I made links. Eventually they were appointed and became an important part of the therapeutic resources available at HMP Holloway. There were times when the art psychotherapists would join the psychotherapy supervision groups and this was an opportunity for us to learn about each other's work. Some women were at a stage where they could make use of art psychotherapy, individually or in groups, and later they may have been able to progress toward undertaking individual psychoanalytic psychotherapy.

I worked closely with the internal probation department. Probation officers were interested in therapeutic interventions with the women. They were keen to help prisoners who had received and made good use of psychotherapy and so had some insights into their offending behaviours and were ready to make changes. Those patients, when they left custody, were keen to be helped to retain the gains they had made while in prison. However, as time went on the resources of the probation service within the prison seemed to be drastically reduced.

Prison officers are the people who have contact with the women most of the time and who respond to their immediate needs. Early in my time at HMP Holloway, at the suggestion of a young and motivated prison officer, I introduced a weekly reflective practice group for them which met for some time. This was open to officers from any unit who were interested in trying to understand and to work with the disturbing feelings being with the women was creating in them. We met in the training department as I felt it was significant that these group meetings be thought of as part of officer training. It was difficult to keep them running on a regular weekly basis as they were often cancelled, ostensibly because of emergencies or problems of cover. Eventually the group stopped. What followed was more individual contact with officers who would share with me and my team the anxieties about the women on their landings.

There was of course a tension for me, between keeping the patient's confidentiality and at the same time responding in a helpful way to the anxiety of the officer, who is having to be with the patient most of the time.

I had close links with the chaplains who were supportive of the therapeutic endeavours of the women and gave psychotherapy a place in the prison. In the early years of my work in HMP Holloway there were a few charitable organisations with a long history of supporting and befriending prisoners. Some approached me for advice as they became interested in providing a therapeutic approach rather than just personal support. I slowly began to believe that psychotherapy had become embedded in the fabric of the organisation.

KR: *How did you go about setting up the psychotherapy service?*
PF: I started assessing patients and quickly I realised there were so many referrals I needed to recruit therapists to develop a service

that would meet the psychological needs in HMP Holloway. I approached psychoanalytic psychotherapy trainings, for example the Portman Clinic, to enquire if they could send student psychotherapists to work in placement at HMP Holloway under my supervision. Recruits had to be in at least once weekly psychoanalytic psychotherapy as part of their course training requirements. Additionally, I required that my trainees had some experience of working in a psychoanalytic fashion. I mean experience of understanding and making use of the transference. Junior trainees would learn from attending weekly supervision and listening in the group to the "verbatims" of sessions delivered by the more experienced psychotherapists and participating in any discussions that arose from that material. So we would speak about transference interpretations made by the therapist and consider what feelings the patients had evoked in her therapist, and sometimes even in the supervision group members. The presence in the supervision group of more experienced psychotherapists was an important part of the learning taking place.

Supervision meetings took place at the same times except for my breaks which were planned in advance. The rhythm of regularity and consistency was very important in containing the anxieties of the psychotherapists, who were exposed to very disturbing material in their sessions. The index offence, that is the offence the women had been found guilty of committing, was always discussed at the start of the therapy. It had to be held in the mind of the therapist; often much more than in the mind of the patient. We tried to speak about the index offence in a non-judgmental way. We thought about it as part of the patient's psychological make up and it was considered central to the psychotherapeutic work.

There were very disturbing feelings in supervision that came in response to violent offences and the concrete way of thinking in the patients. It was also very painful to focus on the emotional and physical deprivation and violent abuse that the patients had experienced in their early and often traumatic lives.

I asked trainees to make a commitment of two years seeing two to four patients per week and a number of trainees, some of whom are contributors to this book, chose to remain working on an honorary and unpaid contract for quite a long time after they had completed their training. They enjoyed the forensic practice and the learning that was taking place for them. Some of them started doing assessments of new patients under my close supervision. I also encouraged some of them to pursue new projects which reflected their interests and their experience, such as setting up the mothers and babies group and the pregnant women group.

In addition to the clinical work I also initiated a monthly forensic forum. This was a discussion and clinical case presentation group open to all professionals involved in the care of the women in HMP Holloway and in other forensic services in the NHS. The speakers would make a presentation about his or her field of specialisation; mostly and often but not always, related or relevant to work with offenders.

KR: *What factors supported or inhibited the development and running of the psychotherapy service?*

PF: One of the main difficulties was my status as a visiting consultant. I had no clear institutional position, and this certainly did affect what I could and could not do. I was never able to have more resources, especially space; psychotherapy suites nor the people to run the service, administrative and secretarial support. This perhaps reflected the ambivalence of the institution to my post and the psychotherapy service. It was only as I started thinking about retirement and planning to leave HMP Holloway that the possibility of securing the psychotherapy service within an NHS trust structure became a reality. At this point, I was replaced by a new consultant forensic psychiatrist in psychotherapy, in much the same way as I had myself been appointed many years before.

I would like to say that, while the lack of a clear institutional position as a consultant was a problem for me personally, at the same time it afforded me the freedom to develop the psychotherapy department in a form I thought was best for that particular institution.

KR: *I am wondering, what was the attitude in the prison and in the outside profession to psychotherapy for female offenders?*

PF: I think we can look at this from various angles. In the first ten years or so I was working at HMP Holloway I had regular contact with the prison governors. There was a new governor every two or three years. They all seemed keen to know about the therapeutic resources for the women in the prison, and specifically about the psychotherapeutic treatment I was offering.

In particular, when I met female governors, they were interested in the women's families and in what was happening to their children. They realised that the psychological help offered to the prisoners could have an impact in the women's families, as often the women in custody were the only parent who had been present in their children's life. The women's problems and their violence, particularly when it was a violent act that had brought them to prison, were acknowledged and there was an interest as well as an expectation that they could be helped to make changes. Officers were also supportive of my work. There were many times when I asked senior officers for help so that a patient could remain in Holloway – because it would have been very disruptive to them if their therapy was suddenly interrupted by a transfer to another prison. Sometimes the transfer would be put on hold so the interruption to the therapy could be discussed, worked with and planned. It also became apparent that sometimes the patient was being moved to a prison that had no psychotherapy provision

These problems became more acute as the number of women in HMP Holloway increased and it became impossible to accommodate their needs. There were times when finding an appropriately furnished room to see a patient was very difficult. It felt as if there was no space for any thinking to take place in the face of pressure from numbers and from the many and various needs of the women.

Dr Estela Welldon, who was a consultant psychiatrist in psychotherapy at the Portman Clinic until the early 2000s, played a big part in bringing attention to the psychological problems of female offenders. The *woman* was largely forgotten as forensic psychiatric and psychoanalytic practice was traditionally focused on men. If we look at the population who commit violent offences, only very few have been committed by women. This was highlighted when I was working at the Portman Clinic, under supervision from psychoanalyst Donald Campbell. I was in a small group of psychotherapists all of whom were seeing only male patients.

I think most of the women who were in prison for a violent offence were referred for psychotherapy very soon after entering prison. These women's crimes were creating difficult feelings for the staff who were working with them. Similar unbearable feelings would be present in the consulting room, in the patient and in the therapist. At those times it felt that the prison setting was very helpful, providing a concrete container for all the feelings and the anxieties which were not possible to contain in one's mind.

In my twenty years working at HMP Holloway, I saw a number of women who had committed violent offences against their children alone or with their partners. I recall a woman who had played a part in the death of one of her children and who was distressed. She worked very hard for a long time in her once-a-week psychotherapy. She had the hope that one day she might be able to care in a safe way for her surviving child. At the end of her time in prison she was admitted to an in-patient therapeutic community where her surviving child joined her some time later. Eventually mother and child were discharged into the community with considerable psychological help and safety measures in place. I think it would be difficult in the present time, with the emphasis on offering brief therapies, to provide the long term therapeutic resources in custody, in the NHS and in the community that this mother needed.

KR: *What specific issues were the women in HMP Holloway bringing? What can you tell me about the attitude of the patients to psychotherapy? Why did they come? What was in it for them?*

PF: Looking back at the beginning of my work in HMP Holloway, I realise that I had felt quite lost in a place where the idea of therapeutic interventions was hardly present. My search for allies in the other prison services proved helpful. Contacts with other departments started and the number of referrals for women from various sources increased. As trainee psychotherapists joined me, they got to know professional people from the other departments in the prison and they kept in touch with services that their patients were involved in. Some of them had previous experiences in their professional lives which they were able to bring in and they developed new therapeutic interventions. It felt as if the fact that I was the only professional person, employed as a visiting consultant without a structure or being part of any prison institutional hierarchy, allowed me the space to develop a service connected to the other services. It allowed new ideas and skills to be present in the department that developed and enriched the service.

I think one of the main differences between the work in the NHS and in prison was in the fact that the women in HMP Holloway were there to spend their sentence. They were away from their families and didn't always know what was happening to their children or their home. This gave rise to a lot of anxiety. Of course some women tried to use the therapy service as a way of moving themselves through the system, but many were motivated to think about the problems that had brought them to prison in the first instance; their violence, their emotional deprivation, and the emotional neglect of their children. Some of these women would take up psychotherapy and work on these painful problems as they hoped they could be different once they were released.

There were women who had committed very violent crimes against children and seemed oblivious to what they had done. These women created a lot of disturbing feelings in the prison officers and other staff working with them. There were particular challenges for the clinical psychotherapy team. Many of the patients were very young and came from backgrounds of emotional and physical deprivation and neglect. Their attachments had been to unreliable parents or carers and their offending was often in the context of violent relationships with men. This made it hard for them to attach to their therapists. There were failures as well as successes.

I remember a woman who had come to England from another country a few years before committing the offence. She would come to her session dressed in a very elaborate colourful dress and with a sort of turban. She would look at me as if what I was suggesting we talk about had nothing to do with her and was of no interest to her. A child who had been left in her care by relatives had died after months of being deprived of food, of warm clothes, of fresh air, of any form of care. This woman seemed to live in a world of her own, with no visible signs of distress and no inclination to speak of this child whose death was her responsibility. She attended for a few meetings but then she stopped coming. I could not do anything to help this woman. But in these sort of situations it is important to support the staff to bear their difficult feelings, so they could continue to care for this prisoner.

I did see for some time a woman whose son had died while in her care at her home while a number of males were also living there. This woman was happy to be offered "help". She would talk about her life with her children as if she and her children had a nice life, making little cakes, playing, going out to the park and visiting the shops. It felt as if the tragic reality of the dead child was left out completely. But it would stay with me. The officers who were looking after this prisoner were struggling with their own feelings, as they were also exposed to all the information about the case coming from the media.

Another example would be a young woman from a small town outside of London who was given a custodial sentence for allowing her baby boy to be harmed by her boyfriend. She had been brought up by a single mother, a professional person, who did not have a partner nor family members or friends involved in her life. The young woman had done well at school until she became a teenager and started going out with boys of whom her mother disapproved. When she became pregnant, she accepted her mother's help for a while. However, eventually she left her mother's home with her baby and moved in with a violent young man who harmed the child. During her stay in prison she was keen to get help and was once again supported by her mother in this. There was a hope that one day she would be able to care for her child. On her release from prison she was supported by a charity and was meant to continue her psychotherapy. This proved difficult as the delay in resuming her psychotherapy was longer than she was able to bear. I maintained contact with her for quite a while and eventually I learned that she had had another baby. It transpired that her mother was now bringing up both the grandchildren together. She had access to her children but only under her mother's supervision.

I think there were many different reasons why women who were referred for psychotherapy would come for the assessment interview and for the weekly treatment. I think some of them were aware that they needed help if they were to bring about changes in their lives. Sometimes they said they felt guilty about leaving their children in the care of their families or fostering and adoption services and not providing for them. Some of them knew they needed to make changes but they did not know how to bring this about on their own. Some of them I recall felt that for the first time in their life another adult person would take an interest in them and would try to help them. They felt cared for even when the therapy work was quite painful.

KR: *How did you measure success with the women, what was a good treatment outcome, and how was this linked to accountability to the criminal justice system?*

PF: HMP Holloway was principally a holding and dispersal centre serving the courts in London and surrounding areas. Women were held on remand as well as serving significant time. Some of the women who were seen for psychotherapy were distressed, as is the case in the NHS or in private practice, and were keen to have help. But the difference is of course that the women in HMP Holloway were judged by society as causing problems for others. As the therapy went on, some were keen to address their problems, and to think about the part they played in the distress they were bringing on themselves, on their families, and to society. Some patients made changes and were keen to make plans for continuing to get help when released. Sometimes we saw the women again when they returned to custody. They may have made some changes though not enough to prevent them coming back into the prison. Sometimes women had been referred to charities offering low fee psychotherapy or the NHS, but few of them would take up those opportunities, often because they could not wait for appointments set long in the future.

I did think about using a self-assessment process for evaluating emotional conditions to measure changes made with the therapeutic intervention as is common in the NHS. However, I decided not to use it with the women in therapy in prison. It was too difficult to apply, as some women would be moved without any prior notice while in therapy, and it would have been impossible to measure the changes made some time after the end of their therapy. I also had no secretarial support and no time available away from clinical work to collate the data. It was perhaps the wrong decision on my part and I later regretted it.

I did consider the outcome of psychotherapies within the service, whether the therapy had ended or whether it had been interrupted by a move of the patient to another prison. I was looking for changes which had taken place in the way the patient's mind worked. Whether the patient was able to take responsibility for her offending behaviour, whether she was able to reflect on her life and whether she had become able to hold onto her thoughts and not to act in a destructive way. A long term follow up of the patient, especially in relation to her offending behaviour, would have been very helpful, had it been possible. I only ever heard by chance about what happened to patients.

KR: *You have described what you consider to be your principal clinical responsibilities at HMP Holloway. How did you integrate your professional goals as a psychiatrist and psychotherapist with the aims of the institution and the wider context of the criminal justice system?*

PF: I held clinical responsibility for all the women who were seen for psychotherapy by myself and the trainees working in my department. I also held final responsibility and accountability for activities involving women, such as groups run by psychotherapists and supervisory work offered by psychotherapists working with me. HMP Holloway was a highly complex organisation sitting within, and influenced by, even more complex institutions; the home office and the criminal justice system. In my mind there were inherent contradictions between security, punishment and reform. I felt from the very beginning that my principal responsibility was to develop the therapeutic dimension for the women during their stay in prison.

I feel as if over many years I did contribute to some of the changes which took place in some of the women who had psychotherapy. I also felt that the prison officers, in part, became more engaged with the women and keen to play their part in facilitating the women's treatment and the work of the mothers and babies unit. The women who end up in prison are damaged and they may damage others. It is important that we in the psychotherapy profession take social and political responsibility for the way they are treated.

KR: *What do you think about the closure of HMP Holloway?*

PF: I felt very sad about the decision to close HMP Holloway. It was rebuilt less than forty years ago to replace the old building on that site. It was still new and modern in comparison with the London prisons for men. In my opinion it could have continued to be a women's prison in London for some time to come. I feel it was important that there was a central London prison with good public transport connections. The location facilitated regular contact between the women and their families, carers and friends. Carers could take children to see their mothers for a daily visit, which were very much appreciated. The family visits were important for keeping contacts between mothers and their children. It seemed to me that prison officers were highly engaged in this part of their work. The expertise of officers and other staff, which had developed over the years, is likely to be lost with the dispersal of the personnel in various prisons in the country. Other professionals, such as psychotherapists and art therapists, who had been engaged in the prison work for a while, will have to look for different settings and new teams. They may or may not be able to fully use the expertise they had gained in HMP Holloway.

I think this book is important in gathering some of what was learned in HMP Holloway so that the learning from there is not lost.

KR: *What did you learn in over twenty years working in HMP Holloway that may be useful to other forensic practitioners and services in existence and yet to be created?*

PF: In theory, I believe the aim of the prison system and my professional goals in the work with the women in prison were the same: helping women who had offended not to offend again. The reality often felt very different. Institutional needs and rules always came first and therapeutic activity had to accommodate that for the service to survive. Most of the therapies offered to the women became time limited; a decision not based in clinical need and appropriateness but rather the increase in numbers of women in custody and the pressure to move women to prisons located away from London. I believe that therapeutic interventions with this clinical population need to be long-term and open-ended in order to make significant changes in the patient's thinking.

Therapeutic resources for women in custody did increase over the years but it became more difficult to offer long term therapies to those women who would have benefited most. There were also problems in trying to set up further help for women when they were leaving custody. This made and continues to make their return to outside life even more perilous with little or no support.

A major factor in criminal offending is the unconscious repetition of familial patterns and there is some circularity in this story. I had decided to leave HMP Holloway and contacted colleagues to organise a replacement in my role heading up the psychotherapy service. I later understood that an email had been sent to all staff announcing my departure and introducing and welcoming my replacement. I was the only person not included into this email.

Nevertheless, we must celebrate our role and responsibility in creating places to think in institutions, even while acknowledging the multiple conscious and unconscious systems that influence both structures and outcomes.

Endnote by Karen Rowe

I met Paola while undertaking my training in forensic psychotherapy at the Portman Clinic in 1999. I felt apprehensive about undertaking a mandatory placement in a prison or special hospital, rather than seeing offender patients in the community as I had been doing of some years. I was unprepared for prison life; the oppressive sense of casual violence, the locking and unlocking of doors, the noise and chaos that filled my ears and my mind, the paranoia of never knowing what was around the next corner.

Under Paola's supervision I worked with women who had seemed to me to be unlucky and unhappy and with others whose cruelty and violence was outside my capacity to understand them and their motives. Paola gave me a guide, a map for understanding the narratives of my patients in the context of the complex and contradictory organisation that was HMP Holloway. I believe Paola's rigorous application of the psychoanalytic method to the practice of psychotherapy with these patients, as well as her recognition of the unique character of the institution and the working relationships around the patient, enabled me and colleagues to do good clinical work and affect sustainable changes. Paola and I continue to work together in peer supervision.

CHAPTER FIVE

Challenges

Working at the boundary of confinement and freedom

Kimberley Wilson

Introduction

The relentless challenges of therapeutic work in forensic and secure settings promote chronic states of anxiety and deprivation. These feelings can provide fertile ground for the development of envy and intense rivalries between clinical teams, as individuals and groups seek to allay anxieties by aggrandising their own work and disparaging the work of others. The complex nature of the patient group means, though, that there cannot be only "one way", and a fragmented team can only replicate the broken histories and inner worlds of the women. This chapter discusses the author's experience and observations of working at and managing the boundaries: staff versus visitor, voluntary versus funded, established approach versus "new wave"; the perils, pitfalls and the progress.

Therapists working in prisons have to navigate a particular set of unique challenges, working in an environment that is anathema to the task of psychotherapy. There is no anonymity; for the client it is common knowledge that they are in therapy, as is the identity of their therapist. The emphasis on security means that there are real and significant limits to confidentiality. The therapist must tread a delicate line between being committed to the patient and being responsible to the prison. These challenges all fall in to a category that I call "border experiences"; the on-going state of being at the boundary between competing demands. Working in this environment one is drawn to dichotomous extremes from the societal level down to the personal and internal. The essential task for the therapist is to recognise the presence and function of these polarities, to make meaning of them and then to find a resolution, or at least a compromise that inevitably demands occupying some space in between these two points.

To work with offenders is to work at the fringes. We work at the edges of society, with patients who have transgressed against society's rules and moral sensibilities. We work with the undesirables; thieves, drug addicts, abusers, murderers. We work with those that others deem undeserving of care and compassion.

Once, at a dental appointment, my dentist asked me what I did for a living. I told him. "Oh", he said without hesitation, "I think those people should be locked up and throw away the key." This professional man, who was otherwise kind and accommodating, was casual about his view that thousands of his fellow citizens, irrespective of the details of their individual crimes, should be left in permanent incarceration. There was no subtlety to his position; he had made a binary category distinction between the people deserving of care (fortunately for me, mouth wide open in his dental chair, that included me) and those who did not. Did he seem anxious about telling me how he felt? Not at all, instead he looked reassured, even righteous.

The environment

I give a lecture on working with female offenders on a postgraduate counselling psychology training programme meters from the former site of Holloway Prison. Some of the students are local to the area. All of them have made the journey over the hill, past the prison in to Camden and central London. Hardly any know the location of the prison. It is invisible. Out of sight and out of mind. This invisibility and the common view of prisoners as espoused by my dentist demonstrate, for me, the function of prison for most of "civil" society. The prison is society's unconscious. As in the individual unconscious it is where the "darkness" resides, the repository for those unpalatable aspects that we cannot or will not witness. There we can cast our own aggression and destructive wishes and turn away, choosing not to see. Collectively we project our own secret violence on to those whose actions have externalised their own inner disturbance. The resolution of this tension begins with being able to turn around and look. To see both inside and out, and find the shared humanity that we each have with any criminal. When we understand that "there but for the grace of God go I" and, undoubtedly, when we have committed to our own introspection, then the work can begin.

Forensic therapists work too at the borders of mental health; our patients have traumatic histories and have gone on to perpetrate trauma. In doing so they act out the humiliation and pain that has become impossible for them to bear. We work at the outer limits of psychotherapy; these are not the so-called "worried well", not people who are otherwise able to function adequately in daily life. These are the uncontained who feel uncontainable. There are multiple comorbidities, at least one – often two – diagnosable mental illnesses, psychotropic medication, criminal justice proceedings, broken families, substance addictions, self-harm and suicidality, hopelessness and distrust. These are patients for whom thinking has become an impossibility, unbearable to the point of destruction. Drugs and alcohol, for this group, are analgesic, killing the pain of the past, the despair of the present, and the presumed hopelessness of the future. They do not want to think. For most, the capability of thinking deeply about the self, an ability derived from internalising the experience of having been thought about, may be impeded. Yet, psychotherapy sits heavily, inescapably at the other end of this see-saw. Thinking is the beginning and the end. Where our patients see it as the problem we contest that it is the solution. Thus, this work can take us to the very edges of our own clinical capacities, our personal resilience and our sense of what therapy "should look like".

The work

I remember an early session with a young woman convicted of a serious offence. I will call her Abbie. She was initially charged with attempted murder but convicted of wounding with intent. She was involved in an argument with a friend. He said something, she "snapped" and instigated this very serious assault. Abbie was referred to me because, soon after her conviction, she became depressed and spoke frequently of suicide. But this was not the gentle, soothing work one might expect with a patient in despair. We could not think about how sad she was or of her multiple losses. Instead she sat for several sessions and told me how shit I was. She told me that I wasn't helping, that I didn't understand and that I never could. Week after week I went to her unit to be told not only that I was useless but that I was making things worse. Week after week I sat in supervision wondering whether she was right. Yet, every week, there she was waiting for me. My function there was not as a thoughtful confidante but as a reliable punchbag, a container for her desperate rage. In those moments when I marshalled myself to take her emotional assaults I was, through the transference, able to comprehend her experience of intimate, persistent physical and emotional violence. Eighteen months later as she prepared for transfer to a lower-security prison she recalled those sessions: "I was a total bastard to you. But you didn't retaliate. That meant everything to me." She would never know what it took for me to make it to the wing during those early weeks, but we were later able to speak about how she needed someone else to experience the humiliation she endured at the hands of her sadistic and violent father. She told me how she wanted someone else to "know what it was like" to be helpless while she – identified with the aggressor (her father, a man who ruled with fear) – inhabited the position of power. This was the violence she exacted during her index offence when the victim used the same crude, pejorative word that her father had used to criticise and humiliate her.

With Abbie, the middle ground between thinking and not thinking was presence. Irrespective of what she thought about me, regardless of what she said, I just had to be there. I had to make clear and undeniable by reliability, my tenacity, toughness (for I had to at least be as tough as her) and my commitment to her. Only then could she develop enough trust or perhaps enough curiosity, to give us both a chance.

The fundamental tension that must be managed when embarking on work in a forensic setting is the internal one. To work in a secure setting is to encounter a philosophical contradiction; that of freedom versus confinement. Our patients are confined because they have been judged to present a danger to society and often to themselves. They have shown themselves to be unwilling or unable to adhere to the mores of general society. Often, as described above, the harms that they exact through their criminal transgressions are symptoms and symbols of the harms that they have been subject to and the solidity of a prison term is the containment that they have been seeking ever since. The experience is of a mind and an emotional world that is out of control, overwhelming and too much for most people to handle. Offenders may feel that they are too much for themselves and their offending procures for them the most secure kind of holding available.

We must begin to understand that on some, not particularly deep, level they *want* to be there. They say to the world, "I need physical restraint", and the world agrees.

In principle, however, psychotherapy disagrees. Psychotherapy consciously says:

> You do need to be held, but we shall do so with words, thoughts and careful attention. With a reliable, thoughtful relationship where you are free to be exactly as you are and, whether that is pleasant or unpleasant, I will be here for you.

The contradiction is that therapy in prison espouses psychological freedom in an environment of physical restraint. The natural position for psychotherapy to take is contrary to confinement; "These places should not exist". Perhaps, when we achieve social utopia this will be so, indeed there would be little need for psychotherapy either. For the present, we resolve this by acknowledging that prison serves an important purpose. Not just as the collective unconscious but as the concrete mother. We do it too by holding in mind that there can be no baby without a mother. Winnicott (1957: 137) tells us, "There is no such thing as a baby . . . A baby cannot exist alone but is essentially part of a relationship." Likewise, there will be no criminal without a victim. Unlike therapeutic work in other settings where the client is the primary focus of our attention, in forensic work we must never allow ourselves to forget or deny that in front of us sits a person who has made a victim of another. As such our responsibility is also to that unknown person, and to society, to invite the convicted person to understand their own minds and actions so that they may be less inclined to act mindlessly in the future. As much as we value freedom we must accept that our patients may not be safe enough to be free of mind nor of body.

Correspondingly, this brings up the question of allegiance. To whom is the therapist's ultimate responsibility? To the patient or the prison? The crucial nature of security is impressed upon you at induction. Any disclosure of an unreported crime, a potential security risk or concerns about emotional states that could result in harm to the self must be reported to staff. This might require the therapist to disclose information about the cause of that distress (an upcoming visit, the anniversary of a death), which in all other clinical environments would remain confidential. This sacrificing of elements of confidentiality is a difficult concession for the therapist but it is essential that the needs and safety of the patient are balanced against the responsibilities of the public and legal institution of prison. Once again the therapist must straddle this uncertain middle ground, which is rarely easy because, though there are some notable exceptions (namely therapeutic communities and secure hospitals), the relationship between the prison and the therapist is ambivalent at best. While this is understandable, especially when movement in therapy exponentially increases the burden on other members of prison staff, it is a blow to one's naïve therapeutic ambitions.

One marker of progress in any therapy is for an otherwise defended patient to begin to connect with deeply denied or repressed emotion. This connection is typically a period of great disturbance. For therapy in the community, realising how angry she is with her parents, a patient may find their regular monthly visits increasingly difficult to tolerate. Recognising that she has chosen her career to satisfy her parents or her peers a patient may find herself irascible in meetings. For offender patients, making this kind of connection is fraught with even greater dangers. Meeting her anger can lead to fights with fellow inmates. Touching deeply buried depressive feelings can provoke self-harm or suicidal behaviour. All of these acts create a security risk for the prison; an increased need for observation, transfer to the separation unit, increased adjudications, perhaps relocation. A prisoner who is undertaking emotional work becomes a more significant emotional burden and security risk to the prison and when this happens the therapist "responsible" for this load is an unwelcome sight on the landing, to both the prisoner patient and the officers on duty. We must find a middle position between being essential for the rehabilitation of the prisoner and being unwelcome to the prison, simultaneously holding on to the value of the work and remembering the – initially, at least – negative consequences of that work on the rest of the establishment. We are denied the gratification of feeling that we are welcome and wanted, either by the patients or the prison itself. This raises important questions about the possibility of unconscious masochistic motivations for therapists choosing to work in such hostile environments.

Deprivation, envy and territory

My time at HMP Holloway taught me much about the realities of deprivation. Every person who enters a prison is deprived: those on remand, the convicted, officers, administration staff, nurses, day care staff, mental health teams; everyone. The deprivation is chameleonic, in that it may be imperceptible and often disguised. But it is there. Like a heavy odour, it hangs in the air, and after a while you get used to it, not noticing until you leave and realise what you have been breathing in all day was far from fresh air. Understanding the complex and pervasive nature of this deprivation allowed me to better comprehend the dynamics of my professional relationships and achieve some success in integrating disparate and sometimes conflicting teams to best support the needs of the women referred to us.

The deprived

Offenders are, by design, deprived of their liberty. Cut off from access to friends, family and home. This is the punishment for the crimes. They are, though, society's deprivation experts, coming as they invariably do with histories of neglect, lack and loss in all forms. Paradoxically, prison is often the place where they are endowed with more than ever before; a secure place to sleep, regular meals, access to primary and specialist care. Yet, this is far from paradise.

Staff are to a lesser extent similarly deprived. Mobile phones and other personal electronic devices are relinquished at the gate. We must be careful not to talk too openly or audibly about our personal lives. Movement within the prison is also, if temporarily, restricted. Staff may not walk in or out freely but must account for their whereabouts, explain their movements, sign in and out should they wish to leave the building. All of this constitutes a loss of a sense of agency and adulthood. By forcing us to account for our whereabouts and watch our Ps and Qs, this concrete mother makes children of us all.

All are deprived by the environment and the "regime", the term used to refer to the daily prison routine. Though Holloway boasted award-winning gardens that offered some respite – an imitation of the natural world in an industrial complex – the ubiquity of walls and gates was inescapable; and with it the anxiety of security. Failure to lock a gate may result in discipline or dismissal meaning that a momentary loss of concentration had serious ramifications. If a prisoner be unaccounted for or there is a miscount on a roll call then the prison is on lockdown; nobody moves, and no one leaves until the numbers add up. The threat of being held indeterminately is a creeping anxiety that sets in as you approach the exit. Unable to leave, unable to let people know you are going to be late, and with no hope of knowing how long it will go on for. In this small way we identified with the prisoners and aspects of their experience of incarceration.

Practitioners in forensic settings are also deprived of the assumption of safety. In other clinical environments we can – broadly but not unequivocally – assume that we are safe. Whether in our consulting rooms or GP clinics we are unlikely to be at risk from our patients, indeed they are probably seeing us because they pose a greater risk of harm to themselves than to us. Working with offenders, particularly those convicted of violent offences, strips from our eyes that veil of safety. We know, without doubt, that the person sitting opposite us is capable of acts of harm and violence, perhaps against people they know well. While one cannot do good work if one is afraid of the patient, there is a legitimate anxiety that accompanies the heightened vigilance of working in prisons.

The envious

The responses to feelings of deprivation are first envy followed by aggressive territoriality; one group makes a claim over an area and defends it against other groups or outsiders. Put another way, when we feel that there is less or little to go around we make greater claims on what we judge to be rightfully ours. The global recession of 2008 has been rapidly followed by a global rise in right-wing and exclusionary politics. We say, if we are in austerity we cannot afford to share what little is left with "outsiders". The oppressive and multi-faceted state of deprivation in prison creates fertile ground for similar territorial skirmishes. As clinical lead for my service I was tasked with managing these dynamics.

I joined HMP Holloway as a trainee psychologist, a junior team member of a new service. There had for over a decade, been a psychoanalytic psychotherapy service staffed by qualified volunteer therapists and led by an experienced consultant psychiatrist. The service I joined had made disquieting ripples having just secured a funded contract to provide both individual and group psychotherapy, alongside providing specialist personality disorder treatment. We were introducing a new service, and new ways of working with offenders with allegiance to a different paradigm, one that was results-focused and evidence-based. It is perhaps not irrelevant to the concepts of competition and envy that the members of the new were also younger than those in the incumbent service. We were, in family terms, the younger siblings and working as we did within a different theoretical orientation it was as if we were half siblings, the children of a new, unwelcome parent. To add fuel to this smouldering fire, the respective leads of the two services, a man and a woman, did not get on well. If the parents were not even speaking to each other how were we siblings to forge a relationship?

There was mutual envy. While the actual amount of funding was modest, being remunerate at all created an immediate category distinction that appeared to say something about relative value. Conversely, the members of the new team knew nothing about the workings of the prison. We did not know the names of the staff or our way around and envied the apparent ease and confidence of the established team. It was soon made clear that the new team was not deemed to be providing "real" therapy. This was an unconscious but vicious attack by the more established team. It felt intended to wound and was successful. The attitude was reflected in missed or late arrivals at joint team meetings, indicating this was not a valuable use of time. In instinctive retaliation, the newer clinicians viewed the psychoanalytic team as "old fashioned" and increasingly irrelevant.

The territorial

The psychoanalytic service had been at Holloway for a long time and they had endured enormous difficulty in establishing themselves within the prison. When they arrived there was little space in the regime for the "soft touch" of psychotherapy. They had their work and their value denigrated, and yet they persisted, securing office space and clearing storage rooms on wings to be used as therapy rooms. With time and substantial effort the team had demonstrated their value to the doubting and suspicious prison. They had fought for their right to be there and earned the respect of the establishment. The challenge of working in such a depriving environment is the difficulty of comprehending one's value. Prior to our arrival the analytic team was valued as the primary providers of therapy in the prison. We would, in the same manner as younger siblings do, benefit from the important groundwork they had laid.

Shortly after starting I was promoted to manager of the team, and it became my responsibility to both ensure my team felt sufficiently supported to do good work and to forge a positive and cohesive working relationship with colleagues in other teams. I am, I think, by nature a pluralist. Just as there is no one experience of depression, there is not one way to work with emotional distress. Different styles, techniques and attitudes will work with different people at different times. It was also true that, in this setting, there was no shortage of people in need of psychological intervention. No doubt, my own experience of sibling rivalry gave me a useful perspective on the disruptive dynamics evinced between the two services. Thinking through the rivalrous dynamics set in motion by the oppressive state of deprivation within the prison took out the sting from the attacks and illuminated the way forwards.

There would be a great deal of satisfaction for me if I could tell you that this integration was achieved through the application of a complex and novel psychological theory, but if I am to develop such a theory, those years are yet before me. Instead, and perhaps serving as an appropriate antidote to an environment so accustomed to hostility, the solution was much simpler. I tried to be nice to people. Not obsequious, but genuinely interested and appreciative of the anxieties they carried with them through the gate.

There was the officer who was, if not exactly cold, then "perfunctory". She did her work, she did it well, but she was largely disinterested in the therapy staff who came onto her wing. She had apparently decided she knew what we were all like and found no common ground between herself and the therapeutic staff. I asked her name and how long she had been there. She told me a couple of years and very soon described how, within the first two days of starting the job she had to respond to a "code blue"; a prisoner had attempted to hang herself and needed immediate medical intervention. "We didn't get any counselling" she stated. She was understandably resentful that as a law-abiding citizen, who was subject to a frightening experience as soon as she started a new job did not received any kind of support or aftercare. Yet the prisoners, who had committed serious crimes, were provided on-going treatment by the likes of me. She was envious of the prisoners in her care. To feel envious of people to whom you feel superior is an unsettling place to be and it is easy to resent both those receiving and those providing the care that is longed for. I let the officer know that I appreciated how frightening an ordeal that was for her and how unfair it was that she and the other officers did not receive sufficient follow-up after responding to a life threatening situation. I offered to raise the issue of support for uniform staff at the next mental health team meeting. I respected her. I valued her contribution. I let her know that, in many ways, her job was much harder than mine. I conceded ground.

Within the prison there was one other counselling psychologist. Symbolically, we were twins; siblings who shared the same identity but who longed to be recognised for their unique qualities. He was working independently, while I was invited to liaise with the in-reach Community Mental Health Team (CMHT). It happened that I was assigned one of his former patients, a young woman with a diagnosis of borderline personality disorder. I agreed a treatment plan with her and the CMHT focused on skills training and observations. One afternoon I went to her wing to meet with her when she told me that she was okay because she had already seen her previous therapist. Though it was disappointing that a colleague would be drawn to act on his own feeling of envy and exclusion so much as to interfere with an on-going treatment, I could understand his unconscious motives. I was moving in on his clinical turf and he moved quickly to re-establish his territory. I suggested that we meet to discuss what was best for this patient and to discuss our working relationship. In a way not dissimilar to the violent woman described earlier, I sat and listened to his complaints. He said that I was unresponsive, that I took too long to respond to his emails. This was not an unfair charge and I told him as much. I apologised for my thoughtlessness and told him that I would not be offended by being reminded of my responsibility to reply. I conceded ground. Nevertheless, this may have been in response to my own feelings that I was intruding on his ground and it is important to observe that prison is filled with unconscious projections being acted out by staff, often concerning feelings of inadequacy and professional value. These inevitably lead to splits between colleagues and may well have been at play in this concessionary dynamic.

Improving the relationship between my service and the psychoanalytic team was a task greater than myself and required a coordinated approach. I met and worked closely with the head of mental health, a woman for whom I still have a great deal of respect and admiration, ensuring that we both had a clear perception of the intergroup difficulties and their underlying dynamics. Like a good mother, she sat her children down and made them talk to each other. The individual team meetings were replaced with one mental health team meeting, compulsorily attended by the heads of all the allied mental health and support services. We outlined the individual strengths and weaknesses of our respective services and cross-referred to each other's teams in a way that was most appropriate to the needs of the women. We agreed to share office space, a small but meaningful concession because sharing physical space inevitably provokes a sharing of mental space, and we were now able to think about each other.

The final verdict

My experience working in what was Europe's largest women's prison was a masterclass of boundary experiences. Consecutively and simultaneously, I found myself treading the line between competing teams, values, and needs. Each day offered a fresh skirmish in the ongoing battle for security, whether that was arguments over space, funding, clinical priorities or, in one case, a patient herself. Key to navigating these complexities was a deep appreciation of how difficult it is to hold on to a sense of one's professional value in the context of deprivation and hostility, and the defences that are mobilised to reaffirm one's sense of worth.

The physical prison structure operates as a brick-and-mortar mother, highlighting its function in physically containing the distress and destructive wishes of the prisoners within it. It was my experience this mother made siblings of us all and these siblings were, at times, warring and fractious until we were able to understand, as siblings do, that we each needed the other, each had an important role to perform and could support one another.

To work in a forensic setting is to work at the boundary of confinement and freedom and to understand the necessity and value of both. It is difficult work that asks for trust from those who have been mistreated and whom mistreat in return, and requires vulnerability from individuals for whom that same vulnerability has been the source of enormous pain. I hope I have shown that within the setting of great deprivation can come something rich and meaningful. It is, for example, testament to Abbie's burgeoning psychological and emotional capacity that, as we approached her release date she spoke about feeling anxious because our work together had been the first experience of real care that she had had. It is also evidence of the good work that can be done in very difficult settings, a testimonial to the long history of painstaking clinical work that went on at HMP Holloway, and of the subtle power of thoughtful persistence; on the wings, in empty dining rooms, in wool shops and association rooms.

In moments of deep silence and door-slamming rage, a therapist sat with a patient and carefully, relentlessly listened.

REFERENCE

Winnicott, D.W. (1957) Further thoughts on babies as persons. In Hardenberg, J. (ed.), *The Child and the Outside World: Studies in Developing Relationships.* London: Tavistock Publications.

CHAPTER SIX

Parallel endings

A personal reflection on the closure of HMP Holloway

Chrissy Reeves

Overview

In 2011 I took over the management of the psychological therapies team in my role as the head of mental health. This was a new and exciting role, which manifested as part of the successful takeover of all the health services within the prison by the NHS trust I was employed by. Prior to this, the health care staff working within prisons were employed directly by the prison service and there was little in the way of governance or guidance. There was a confusing myriad of different providers.

I had been working in the prison for three years up to this point, on loan from the NHS, managing the health care assessment unit. This was essentially an acute mental health unit within the prison. In addition, I managed the day centre and an occupational therapy team attached to the assessment unit. Although these looked like general mental health services at first glance, it was impossible to forget that they were "inside". They were staffed jointly by health and prison staff and the rules around what could be done for the patients were decided by prison security. Although I was nominally "in charge", there were constant reminders of where the true power and authority lay.

There were some aspects in which the patients themselves were similar to those found in general mental health services. However, there were many clear differences: these women had more physical health problems and addictions were common place. Many were lacking in social skills and education and few had enjoyed opportunities or support. It is important to understand the serious challenges faced by staff working with a prison population, attending to women whose lives were blighted by abuse, addiction and poverty. Violence was often the norm. The fight just to survive was a daily struggle for women who had experienced violent relationships, homelessness or work on the street.

The prison

Holloway was the largest women's prison in Europe with an operational capacity of nearly six hundred. Demolished in the 1960s, the old Victorian jail, which had looked like a castle, was replaced by a faceless concrete block near the Holloway Road in north London. The thinking around the new building was that it should incorporate a hospital layout. Gone was the traditional panopticon style that had been popular in institutional architecture since the nineteenth century. Indeed "the trolley route" was the main thoroughfare around the prison until the day it closed. This route was designed to be wide enough to wheel through a hospital bed and had the appearance of a hospital corridor with bumpers around the walls. For many working in health care at the time, the psychological thinking was that female offenders were ill and needed care. Many saw women as mad, not bad, unlike their male counterparts.

The primary task of any prison is to keep the inhabitants securely under lock and key to protect the general public. Those individual incarcerated must be kept safely and decently and work must be done towards their rehabilitation when they rejoin society. The primary task of health staff working with patients is to promote health and to provide care and treatment when clinically indicated. These two different, sometimes opposing, tasks created conflict and confusion. Unifying these primary tasks was not easy. There were frequent occasions when health absolutely needed to come first and security assessments did not always allow it.

I always kept in my mind that security staff could not do their work without health care. To me it seemed obvious the women needed to be well enough to manage the regime. To keep a prison running there must be routine, consistency and rules that are adhered to. Many of the staff came from military backgrounds and were used to the discipline of regimes. Generally, health staff had different kinds of backgrounds. They often had to think creatively to respond to the challenges they were presented with and could be more flexible in their approach. The prisoners themselves were mostly chaotic and came from lives with few rules or standards.

From the health care perspective, the first thing to do with new staff is remind them that they are in a prison. By this I mean that ultimately they are not in charge of their charges. They may develop a wonderful care plan providing the individual with the best treatment to meet her needs. But that woman may not even be living in the same cell, wing or prison by the time you come back to see her the following week. If for example, a conscientious mental health nurse decides to read the National Institute for Health and Care Excellence (NICE) guidelines for managing self-harm, they will notice that many of the techniques recommended are just not possible for those who are incarcerated: going for a walk is not possible, removing oneself from a situation is not possible, even providing stationery to use as a distraction is not possible. These items could be contraband and you might find yourself accused of being conditioned by the prisoner to smuggle items into the jail.

When the prison staff are trained they learn all the instructions and the orders. They are supported by a hierarchy of seniors in order to keep the rules and do things right. Then in come the "civilian staff" who try and do it all a different way. This inevitably causes conflict. Prisoners are quick to see the differences and can be very adroit at splitting professionals. As a civilian, you are reminded of your status as a guest in the establishment, however senior you may be. Keys can be taken away from you if you step too far out of line. There is always a threat of being "walked to the gate" if your blunder is considered serious.

The women's health

There is no denying the inequalities in health when comparing the prison population in the UK and that of the general public which cannot be emphasised enough. Sadly, it remains unacknowledged or believed by many. The prisoners at Holloway had far greater needs relating to substance misuse, mental and physical health, including dentistry and medication, than the general population. Eighty per cent of the women took prescribed medication. Administering this to the population within dedicated time limits every morning, noon and night was a difficult task as the prison regime took precedence over health care.

Many of the women were incarcerated for drugs offences and petty non-violent crimes. They were in prison for short periods of time; sixty per cent were imprisoned for less than six months. One television programme made at Holloway during this period highlighted a particular woman who said she intentionally came to prison in order to detox from drugs and to have a full health check. The prisoner said this was the only way she could see out of her situation in the community, where treatments were not available. Women preoccupied with drug use do not take care of their physical health. They are usually smokers, who spend any money they have on their addictions, often meaning that dietary intake is neglected. Often they are underweight with dental problems due not only to poor dental hygiene but also to the sugar levels in the prescribed opiate substitute methadone.

Not all prisoners come into prison choosing to detox from the substances they are addicted to. In this respect substance misuse services in prisons are unlike any equivalent services in the community where individuals can only access them by choice. In prison, individuals are detoxed whether they like it or not. This obviously creates challenges for relationships between the prisoners and staff. Women, without their crutch, can find their feelings overwhelming: the drug use having enabled them to ignore their previous experiences of trauma, guilt and shame. Many women inside are dismissed as "medication-seeking", without attempts to understand the context from which this behaviour is driven. The detox policy itself creates mental ill health. Many women come into prison with mental illness. Anecdotally it felt like this was on the increase over the years. This is no surprise when one stops to review the reduction in funding to mental health services. We found the women with the most challenging problems were often "banned" from community mental health services due to their behaviour or discharged due to their non-engagement. As external services reduced their bed capacity and developed stricter rules about violence to staff, the group of women we were expected to treat grew ever larger. Prison began to fill the gap left by mental health funding cuts. On the health care assessment unit approximately two-thirds of the population were in the process of transfer to hospital under the mental health act for treatment at any time. The remainder accepted treatment and became well enough to return to the main prison or they were released from custody directly from health care because the transfer process had taken so long or because they would never be well enough to manage the prison regime.

The limits of management

Prison health care services are services like no other. They are commissioned to provide equivalent services to those found in the community. However, the population has increased compared to the average caseload found in a GP practice. As well as the health inequalities, the behaviour of the patients could be extreme and the context of the environment meant that patients could not always be accessed. The management, I include myself in this group, meant well and made every effort to support the health needs in the best way they could. Despite this, there was always a lot of criticism of the health care staff; from the women themselves, from the prison staff, the Independent Monitoring Board, and inspectors.

The culture when I entered the service was certainly one of blame. If anything went wrong and it could be blamed on health care it inevitably was. The officers were used to saying to each other and anyone within earshot that the nurses were "shit" and didn't know what they were doing. Health care staff were critical of one another. Perhaps prison health care had been poor in the past. When health care staff were employed directly by the prison there were no governance structures. Training and support for these staff sat completely outside of the wider NHS. Prison health care had been the place where those people went to work who could not get jobs anywhere else. They were then consistently neglected and blamed by the institution when things went wrong.

Management therefore had quite a task on their hands. Some managers were forward thinking and dynamic, others more careful and slower in their approach. Both styles brought successes and problems. If prison governors did not get the response they wanted there and then, they just went and found another manager. Boundaries were blurred, hackles raised.

My own management style seemed to work in this environment, in part perhaps because I am naturally a people pleaser. It is important to me to be liked and for people to think highly of me. I was motivated and wanted to do a good job, for the women and for the health care staff. I was also keen to support the prison staff as much as possible. I became a mediator between strong personalities, the sense maker when situations could not find a way forward and the container for the anxiety of others. My door was always open. I knew about the women and the staff I managed. Staff from other teams, within health, probation, charities and the prison came to me with their challenges about work and their lives outside. However, I was frustrated with my senior managers throughout my time at Holloway. All three over this period had different styles and I found them all unsatisfactory. In fact, I wanted to be in charge overall myself but was not given this opportunity. I was highly ambitious and felt held back.

The psychological therapies service

In summary, health services in prisons provide equivalence of care in the community to a population of people who are more disadvantaged than any community population. It stands to reason then that there is a great need for psychological intervention. With many talented and committed therapists on hand we were extremely fortunate at Holloway. Nevertheless, it was a battle to provide this service right up until the end. When I took on the management of the psychological therapies (PT) service it was in disarray; not one collective service at all. There were many different groups of people providing psychological interventions from different contexts, funders, and to different groups of women.

Firstly, there was a consultant psychiatrist in psychotherapy with a team of mainly honorary forensic psychotherapy trainees. This very experienced professional had her own office, a rare and prized space in such a chaotic and crowded institution. Having worked in Holloway for many years her standing within the establishment and the wider psychotherapeutic field was strong. This team's work was mainly with the more serious offenders, assessing their state of mind at the time they committed their offences and offering psychodynamic or analytic psychotherapy to those who were able to take this up.

Secondly, there was a limited company providing psychological interventions via a paid group of staff: psychologists, dialectical behavioural therapists and psychotherapists. However, just prior to my appointment the company had gone bust. I was not privy to the detail but knew the staff group had been kept on and were now offering interventions as the "primary mental health team". These therapists worked with individuals whose needs were less complex; those women experiencing anxiety and depression for example. My initial observation was of a considerable rivalry between these two psychotherapy providers.

Thirdly, there was the art therapist whom I had managed since she started working within the prison in the day centre. We quickly found that this was not the correct place for her and challenges arose as art therapy was misunderstood by the occupational therapy team and senior management. It was wonderful to have the funding for the post and the agreement that non-verbal therapeutic work was required. As soon as the opportunity arose I expanded the role and the art therapist joined the PT. Here her work could be better supported by colleagues with similar psychodynamic training and concerns.

There was also a charity who worked solely with women who had experienced child loss. This was a well-used service that had great relationships with officers and a steady stream of referrals. Many prisoners experience the loss of a child. This may be through miscarriage, children taken into care or adopted, or separation from children due to imprisonment. What became apparent very quickly with this team was that they were taking referrals from throughout the prison. Anyone could make a referral, including the women themselves. Offering their programme to those who had killed or abused their own children was problematic and it was questionable whether this was the most suitable treatment. It was agreed therefore, that this charity should join the PT service.

We were lucky to have a fifth psychological service also from another well-known, well-respected and well-established charity: Women in Prison. They provided counselling for prisoners who experience domestic or sexual violence. Their interventions were through group and individual work and the manager of this service was clear from the outset that she wanted to be part of the PT team.

The bringing together of these five strands of psychotherapy seemed obvious to me. It was clear the fragmented way of working was not helping the teams, the women, the reputations, or the rest of the staff in the prison. Despite the teams all doing great work independently they didn't really know anything about the function of the others and the women didn't understand what the differences were in the interventions offered. The prisoners and the officers understood the words counsellor, psychologist and therapist only vaguely and if they didn't like what one professional was doing they just sacked them and got another. This led to further splitting between teams and the lowering of reputations and understanding alongside professional suspicion and rivalry due to a lack of communication and boundaries. A few particularly astute women managed to have up to three professionals working with them at any one time, while others languished on the waiting list indefinitely. The most complicated women, often personality disordered and high profile, seemed to be successfully playing the professionals off against one another. Security and other prison staff frequently became embroiled in the "sacking" of a therapist and issues around confidentiality were chaotic and confusing. When a therapy patient tells an officer that her therapist "said that I have to talk about my offence but if I do I'm going to end up hurting myself or someone else", the resulting decision is that the therapeutic relationship was a security risk by the prison. Without attempting to seek another perspective, a new referral would be made to another team deemed a softer or safer option.

Here we had five therapy teams. Some therapists were highly experienced with many years of forensic work under their belts. Other therapists were also supportive, compassionate and helpful but perhaps less aware of the complexity of working in the prison environment and the risk of unconsciously colluding with the prisoners. The therapists struggled to come together and there were multiple referrals for the women who were causing the most difficulties in the prison leading to multi-professional involvement. There was no forum for discussion about who or which team was the most appropriate for the individual. Only one therapy team had a professional office for weekly supervision in addition to a dedicated, well-cared for therapy room. Combined with not knowing what the other therapists were providing there was an unhelpful amount of envy and suspicion, destructive emotions which reflected the prisoners own relational and material envy.

The clinical work itself took place in a variety of settings, some in the dedicated therapy room, some in group rooms and some in cells. The provision of therapy in prisons does not necessarily replicate that in the community. Therapists would go to the wings to find their patient and if she was not there the therapist might look for her and gently enquire why she had not attended her session. This might sound unsettling to a therapist in private practice. However, forensic patients may often need to be looked for, to be lost and found in an unconscious attempt to feel valued and kept in mind by the therapist. The game of hide and seek usually settles down after the initial efforts of the therapist who stands up for the therapy by putting effort and thought into finding and thinking with her patient. Finding out why a patient "forgot" to attend a session may reveal rich material with which to work. In a way for me this was the beauty of prison work. It is systemic. Even when working with individuals, one cannot just take information straight from the horse's mouth. The wider system informs as to what is going on. Staff on the wings were happy to talk about how the individual was getting on and tell the therapist how the patient was managing between sessions. The therapy at Holloway was untraditional in this respect and in many ways the institution supported the work. Unlike in the community therapists could locate their patients. This allowed women to make use of treatment and access therapy in a way they could not manage in the community. It was deeply rewarding over the years to see what good use very damaged and deprived women made of psychotherapy – so often dismissed as a self-indulgent process for the worried well.

Pulling the strands together

My ambition was to make sure therapy could be offered in a more organised and transparent way. I was aware that one of the rooms available to health care was large. It had a meeting space as well as computers and I decided that all the therapists and myself would meet here for a weekly referral meeting. I insisted this meeting would happen for one hour every week to discuss every referral that came through to any of the five teams. This would allow the referral to be allocated to the most suitable treatment and put an end to the overlapping of services. Together we could manage a waiting list and streamline the existing caseloads. All the therapists were part time, but many were in Holloway on specific days for supervision. This day was chosen for the referral meeting and I made it mandatory to attend.

I was nervous before the first meeting. Everyone was being very nice to me. As the new manager I had taken time to sit down and meet with most of the teams individually. I had listened to how they worked, their frustrations, what was great about the work and why they stayed. However, I detected an undercurrent of dissatisfaction, distrust, and slight paranoia, as is often the case in prison settings. I admit now that I was unsure whether anyone would turn up to this meeting but they did. Everyone attended and I began with an explanation as to why this had to happen and how I foresaw the team developing.

I stepped into this meeting and the overall management of this team from a perspective of appreciative inquiry. I assumed the best from this group of people. I started with the idea that they would all want the team to be a success and that together we could grow and provide an excellent service. I was right about this. Nevertheless, although everyone seemed to want the best for the service and the women outwardly, I wondered if there were some who did not. Perhaps some wanted to see the service fail, preferring to hear people reflect back on the good old days. This was not a view ever explicitly stated by anyone, but it was a feeling that I held. Perhaps I was picking up on unconscious projections from some of the team members. I try to be empathic and I suspected this unspoken desire was more than a paranoid thought in my own head.

Over time we developed a successful model of work: one referral form for the whole service, all referrals discussed, individual referrals allocated for assessment then presented back to the meeting and finally, allocated to a suitable therapist for work to begin. Everyone had clinical supervision in groups. We quickly reduced the waiting list to zero. We developed therapy groups, some working collaboratively with other parts of the service: substance misuse, mental health, and primary care. The work was systemic, with therapists working together with the team around the individual. This might include housing, probation and families as well as other parts of the health service. The work was rich and plentiful. I feel proud of what we achieved.

Despite this, success wasn't easy. Some of the staff moved on. Some left by choice taking new jobs or retiring. Others went because we needed to lose them. Change is difficult and this cannot be understated. The changes in this team were huge. Not everyone coped with the transparency, the collaboration, the clinical note-writing. Many things that as a nurse managing a mental health team were second nature to me, felt uncomfortable for psychotherapists and counsellors who had not been used to working in this more joined up way. Prisons are very complex institutions. To work in silos, in isolation, without taking into consideration the individual's world around them seemed like a dangerous fantasy to me.

As I have reiterated throughout this chapter, working in a prison is far from easy. Mental health concerns clash with the notions of punishment. Many of us felt strongly about the system we were working in. At times it felt harsh and unjust and there often seemed to be a lack of thinking about the impact of what happened day to day on the prisoners. For example, excellent projects were funded to support women with autism and personality disorder, only to disappear when the funding stream ended. Regardless of how well the project had done, the service would be withdrawn and the women on the caseload would experience yet another thoughtless abandonment or be retraumatised as a result of the system. I have wondered what attracts us to work in such a punishing system, what it is in our own valency that brings us in. Consciously we have a desire to make a difference, to do important work, but ultimately we are left feeling damaged by it ourselves. We then feel surprised that this should be so without imagining that the institution impacts all of its inhabitants.

The ending

Having worked so hard to create a community, only to lose it, I am left thinking mostly about the prison staff and the women. I have thought about Sinek's (2016) description of millennials in the workplace to inform these thoughts. He describes millennials and their need for instant gratification via the use of phones and social media. These are not available to those on the inside. Phones and other technology are all locked away for the duration of staff shifts and from the residents for the entirety of their incarceration. Sinek tells us that what millennials fail to realise is that satisfaction at work and deep meaningful relationships cannot be instantly achieved. For these things to be successful, people need time, connection and focus. This is something that in prison can be found in abundance. What does time enable? Relationships to grow, friendships to emerge, networks to be forged. Trusted people you can get to know and rely on if there are incidents and you need the support of others. The women developed relationships with one another and with the staff that were meaningful and unexpected.

In November 2015, when the news came that Holloway was to close and this peculiar prison family was to be dismantled and broken up, there was a sense of fear and chaos.

I had already resigned from my position a week prior to this announcement in the House of Commons. As I have said; I was ambitious. I wanted to be in charge of the whole of health care. I was dissatisfied with my senior management. I felt held back from achieving more successful services for the women. Instead I felt locked in, imprisoned myself. The services I ran were in good order, with high standards, meeting all the key performance indicators (KPIs). There was room for creativity and further development and we were working towards this.

I had done some work in the other departments, supporting the managers there, but this was no longer considered my responsibility when my new manager arrived. In fact, those services stopped doing some of the work I had implemented because "it wasn't in the health care contract"; the communication being that if it was not required or measured we don't do it. It did not seem to matter if it was good for the women, the staff or the morale. Nor did it seem to matter that these services were performing well, meeting their KPIs and fully staffed despite being considered difficult to recruit and retain to.

My ambition was not welcomed. I felt put in my place. The new manager saw no need for me to attend external meetings as she went to them all. So I became a prisoner from Monday to Friday. This felt like a reflection of the women's experience. They too lacked opportunities and had to fit into a rigid regime that may have felt empty and alien to them. If they were able to feel ambition, it was rarely nurtured and although the staff hoped they would not return to custody no one was surprised when they came back. Many women described feeling trapped, sad and angry at their situations and I soon came to feel this way.

Having spent a number of years building up strong teams with good leaders I now felt under occupied and overlooked. We had worked together to problem solve and develop the mental health team and had created flexible and responsive services. Unlike other parts of the service we had no vacancies. Every job we advertised attracted high calibre staff who knew what they were applying for and were committed. I had left myself space as the deputy head of health care to step into the other services only to be told that I was surplus to requirements. In an institutional mirroring, the women too were under occupied and overlooked. The operational capacity had increased over the years, yet the number of jobs, training courses and education spaces had not. All sentenced prisoners were required to attend "purposeful activity" during the day or they were penalised. Stuck in my office I did research and development activity but ultimately I started to lose my confidence and feel less useful.

Prison health care is contracted out by NHS England; one of the first health services to be subject to tendering with many now run by private providers. During the last year of my work the service was up for re-tender. I had some input into putting this together, but ultimately it was mainly written by senior management. It occurred to me in the autumn that I hadn't seen the final version that had gone in for submission. I asked my manager if I could see it. She brought it up on her computer screen. She showed me the staffing charts for each part of the service. I was not included. My position had been deleted. I had not been informed.

Prisoners can be moved around the country and across establishments at the will of the prison service. These decisions may be made according to capacity issues, behaviour management or the availability of training programmes. Prisoners do not always have notice of this. They may get up in the morning only to be told they are now on a transfer list and should pack. Perhaps we can acknowledge that prisoners have three basic needs; somewhere to live, something to do, and someone to care for. My senior management team removed all of these things from me in my work. No one acknowledged the quality of the work I had done. No one had the guts to actually tell me what was going on. No one in the senior management team ever discussed what was happening with me. Looking now at how the prisoners and staff were treated it seemed as if systemically what happens in the wider environment was happening on a micro level inside the institution. Fiscal concerns had trumped integrity or compassion.

In this instance my employer did not win the re-tendering contract. I resigned. Then government announced the prison was closing. I fell apart during my three month notice period. This was not noticed by many people. I'm very good at the British stiff upper lip in public. However, I was not able to offer my staff the same level of containment and support that I had done previously. I leaned more on them and some couldn't handle this. Their "mother" was losing control. This may have been frightening and upsetting for them as they struggled with their own chaos. The family was being separated and to see all we had built together being destroyed and disbanded for financial gain was very painful. Women who have been incarcerated often describe feeling deeply affected by their experience. I find now that I am left marked by the work; scarred.

REFERENCE

Sinek, S (2016) *Start with Why: How Great Leaders Inspire Everyone to Take Action*. London: Penguin.

PART III

LIVING IN PRISON

CHAPTER SEVEN

Living and dying

A journey through the life cycle of the Onyx art therapy group for women from overseas

Siobhan Lennon and Zoe Atkinson

Introduction

This chapter takes the reader on a journey through the life cycle of the Onyx art therapy group; from its conception and birth, through adolescence and mid-life and on to the group's "twilight years" and eventual death. Using vignettes from various points in the group's life cycle, the authors seek to reflect the experiences of some of the women who participated in the art therapy group and to describe processes at work from the therapists' perspectives.

Background

Onyx was established to offer group therapeutic provision to women prisoners at HMP Holloway who held the status of "foreign nationals". This term refers to prisoners whose passport is non-UK. They accounted for up to 30 per cent of the population at Holloway, far higher than the 12 per cent in the average prison population in England and Wales (Prison Reform Trust, 2016). This higher number was a reflection of Holloway's location, situated in the diverse city of London.

An art therapy group for "foreign nationals" at Holloway provided a means of working with a complex, multi-layered group within the prison. The women who attended and the wider foreign national population were not a homogeneous group. However, they faced similar challenges of being marginalised and unseen. They were often unfamiliar with the bureaucratic system and prison culture, and largely disconnected by language and cultural barriers. The stigma of being labelled a "foreigner", "asylum seeker" or "illegal immigrant" was an additional obstacle. Separation from family and friends intensified feelings of isolation and loneliness. The on-going reality of possible deportation was a constant presence in the lives of many of the women who attended the group.

Prisons are social constructs (Foucault, 1977), inextricably woven into the fabric of society. They function as part of a complex justice system and serve to contain a part of society deemed anti-social, non-compliant or dangerous; both on a conscious and unconscious level. Considering the high levels of neglect, trauma and abuse experienced by the women who populate prisons (Corston, 2007) Suzanne Delshadian poses important questions when she asks:

> what does society demand of prisons ... what is the institution asking its therapists to contain on behalf of society? The prison as an institution is being asked to operate on limited resources, contain the conflict within and – if possible – also provide treatment and change. All this, without making too many demands on society.
> (Delshadian, 2003: 72)

Onyx ran over the course of fifteen months until shortly before the closure of HMP Holloway in summer 2016. The group met once a week for a session lasting two and a half hours. This was a lengthy duration for a group session which sometimes felt unhelpfully long. Nevertheless, the group had to accommodate the prison regime, materially demonstrating the conflict which exists between the security function of the regime-focussed prison and the interpersonal focus of the therapeutic intervention.

Birth

Following a protracted conception during which the need for an art therapy group for women prisoners from overseas was identified, Onyx was born and given a name. Its birth comprised a room, two art therapists, a supervisor, four group members, art materials and an expectation that something important might take place; the group would grow and this growth would be navigated by those who took part. The women who attended were referred for group treatment for a multitude of reasons and presented with varying levels of need, capacity to relate, and ability to use what was on offer.

Some participants functioned well within the prison, while others were deemed isolated and there was concern for their physical and mental wellbeing. Some women were pregnant, some were already mothers and grandmothers. For one particular woman, Maya, there was great anxiety throughout the prison regarding her mental health and level of self-harm. Maya had arrived at Holloway having spent time in prison abroad. She had been convicted of importing drugs and given a lengthy sentence. Over time Maya became a constant in the group, a culture carrier and integral cog in the group dynamic. For Maya, and others, being part of an art therapy group was a containing experience (Bion, 1986). The group created a space in which it became possible to feel and explore overwhelming and destructive feelings in relative safety and in relation to others. Caroline Case describes how art therapy can offer containment and how image making can become a realm for exploration when she says, "Images have the possibility of holding many varied meanings simultaneously at quite different levels of experience. The finished image can be a vehicle for exploration of both inner and outer worlds" (Case, 1999: 83).

Images and art making can be seen, felt and read on multiple levels. Meanings can be multifarious as well as homogeneous and reliance on a shared verbal language is not always necessary. Offering art therapy in prison, to a group of women who were holding together fragmented selves under conditions of immense stress, was a means of creating a containing environment that offered the possibility of feeling understood.

In the early stages of the group there was enjoyment, experimentation and even delight in using the art materials which were explored both tentatively and dramatically (Figure 7.1). This could be likened to the early stages of child development. The baby explores through play and both infant and parent may delight in this, creating a bond of care (Winnicott, 1964). As the weeks went by and the group developed, a stronger, more explicit connection began to emerge between art making and feeling. This was clearly observable during one session when Maya arrived at the group in distress, describing past experiences of abuse, cruelty and neglect. Although Maya had spoken of her traumatic history before, on this occasion her words were disturbing and conveyed her

Figure 7.1

active wish to commit suicide. Maya went on to create art work which felt flat and disconnected from the trauma she was communicating. Meanwhile, the group became intensely busy. A family was drawn with heavy black outline and soon became swamped by a shifting landscape, flooded with a complex weather system of rain and storms. Slowly, in stages, a rainbow emerged as the rain appeared to stop and dry up. It seemed as though Maya's intensely painful and overwhelming feelings were identified, explored and processed through the art making of others in the group, while Maya herself could not make the connection. During the final moments, the group became heavy and floppy and laid their heads down on the table, perhaps exhausted by this intimate unconscious exchange. Freud recognised these unconscious communications when he wrote, "It is a very remarkable thing that the unconscious of one human being can react upon that of another, without passing through the conscious" (Freud, 1915: 198).

Childhood

Some women arrived at the group eager to be creative and make their own choices. It seemed important for some that their creativity was self-directed and the therapists were not "telling them what to do".

LIVING AND DYING   105

Food was frequently discussed as a means of expressing culture and identity, colours and materials were chosen and stories were shared. At times it seemed as though a "family" was being built, oscillating between harmony and discord, support and rivalry. The group population shifted frequently. There were new admissions and when release dates came some women left the prison, while others were moved to immigration removal centres in preparation for their deportation back to countries they may have left many years ago. Some women in the group just waited while their cases meandered through the legal system. The women's future journeys were discussed with feelings of fear, anxiety and sometimes resignation. At times artworks were made which seemed to be in preparation for these onward journeys (Figure 7.2).

One day Maureen arrived in the group. Maureen was serving a sentence for immigration fraud and was facing possible deportation after completing her time. Maureen was a quiet and patient presence in the room and would often speak about her experiences in prison being like nothing she had experienced in her life outside. Maureen frequently referred to her faith and wrote motivational poems reflecting her beliefs. Her poems seemed to be created with the intention

Figure 7.2

to lift and guide the group and perhaps herself. Both therapists' countertransference towards Maureen was experienced as heavy, opaque and foggy and held a sad, depressive quality. Outside of the group the therapists thought about their countertransference and questioned what it might be like for Maureen, a woman in her sixties, to be in prison awaiting deportation. Did her offence really warrant this punishment or was Maureen actually a "good fairy-grandmother", sent to raise the spirits of the group. Feelings of injustice were stirred-up for the therapists and they were reminded in supervision of the potential of colluding with the powerful feelings of unfairness contained within prisons (Teasdale, 1995).

Maureen's depictions of houses emerged in the first session she attended. Initially seen from the air, as though viewed from a plane or from the heavens, Maureen's house was a structure without windows or doors (Figure 7.3). Maureen's next house differed somewhat, this time with an open doorway and viewed from the ground (Figure 7.4). Maureen had collaged a jagged, rocky looking surface from pieces of red felt which she described as "a red carpet which will pave my footsteps when I leave prison". The carpet looked uneven with gaps and odd-fitting shapes. The therapists

Figure 7.3

Figure 7.4

wondered if Maureen's path would be as smooth as she imagined. By her seventh session Maureen's house was being collaged from wooden matchsticks. These materials were more substantial than the thin pre-cut card she had used initially; more solid, three-dimensional and real. Furthermore, they required Maureen to build; measuring and planning out the size and shape of her house. Perhaps through these images Maureen was also building her "inner house" and strengthening her "internal materials". We were reminded of Case's (1999) earlier description of art therapy and the image in relation to inner and outer worlds.

As the summer advanced the prison gardens blossomed and the temperatures inside rocketed. The group came to a planned break while the therapists sought external funding to allow it to continue. They were unsure if the group would resume in September and this ending held with it an air of uncertainty. This insecurity mirrored the experiences of the women who had been in the group; uncertain of their futures and awaiting decisions from unreachable, external departments. Over the previous six months the group had formed, identified a primary task (Bion, 1961) and developed a sense of itself through what could be thought of as a long childhood.

Adolescence

Funding was secured and after six weeks the therapists resumed the group for a further eight months. The uncertainty of its future may have been felt by group members as another unreliable, unsafe relationship with the potential to break down. Perhaps this was also experienced as a negation of care from the therapists; reminiscent of previous experiences of being let down by those in positions of trust and authority.

Maya, Maureen and others returned along with newly referred women. Maureen quickly began work on another house. This time it became a three-dimensional sculpture, a home complete with garden, front yard, chimney and door (Figure 7.5).

Figure 7.5

Maureen worked diligently on her house, returning week after week to continue her project. The group were curious and asked questions, but Maureen's responses gave little away, "I will speak about it when I'm finished" she told them. However, the group's questions remained unanswered and Maureen's house was left incomplete as she was unexpectedly transferred to an immigration removal centre in preparation for her deportation. Maureen's house-sculpture remained, a reminder of her disappearance and absence from the group. Edwards (1997) reflects on the subject of loss and sorrow in relation to artworks left behind by patients and the feelings of sadness, regret and guilt when remembering the left behind pieces and lost relationships. He connects these feelings to the process of grief and mourning.

In the following weeks the room became busier as more women joined the group. At this time some of the artwork seemed to begin to communicate emptiness. Decorative boxes lay bare and empty inside, cards had shiny decorative fronts but nothing written within. There was much wrapping and covering, sticking of patterned papers and making of decorative accessories. The previous playful, childlike delight of creative discovery was seemingly replaced by an inner emptiness, outwardly communicated by these empty boxes and blank cards. Doubts about the group were verbalised; "What am I doing here?" "Is coming to this group helping?" and themes of despair and hopelessness surfaced. A woman brought the myth of Pandora's Box to the group, but her version was sketchy and incomplete. She was unable to find or remember the hope which remained in the bottom of Pandora's Box.

This emerging sense of hopelessness and questioning could be likened to a stage of adolescence whereby ambivalent feelings surface and there is a desire to break away from the familial group and the primary task (Bion, 1961). At this point in the group's development, perhaps in response to the potentially painful feelings that were being expressed, an aggressive, gang-like behaviour emerged. A group member described as a "prolific offender" came to fulfil the role of gang leader, supported by some close allies. The gang brought with them raucous discussion of prison life, drugs and sex. Attitudes became more predatory, aggressive and confrontational. As the parental couple and figures of authority, the therapists were challenged and denigrated in their attempts to create some thinking space within the group (Bion, 1961), which at times felt threatening. Psychotherapist Hamish Canham describes gangs and a gang state of mind as, "essentially anti-parents, anti-life, and anti-thinking" (Canham, 2002: 115) He goes on to describe gang behaviour as "a simple solution to the pains involved in having ambivalent feelings" (ibid.: 116).

This aggressive communication threatened the quieter spaces and participants in the group. Some women, unable or unwilling to join the gang, were pushed out to the edges of the group. Some chose to leave. This created anxiety for the therapists as they questioned their responses and ability to survive the attacks (Bion, 1959) and keep the group together.

Maya continued to openly share her vulnerabilities within the group, demonstrating her lack of awareness to the danger presented by the gang state of mind (Canham, 2002). In contrast, other women disguised their vulnerabilities and needs through aggression; displaying their superior abilities or scapegoating others. Conflict and hierarchy seemed to be evident in some of the artwork made at this time (Figure 7.6).

For some women art-making seemed difficult and exposing, seeming to convey an admission of vulnerability. Feelings of dis-satisfaction and unfairness surfaced and became a focus. At this time there were strong suggestions that the therapists and group were not providing "enough". The group seemed to be verbalising feelings that may have related to a failing maternal function (Winnicott, 1965) and the perceived failure of the therapists to keep the whole group safe from the gang state of mind.

Furthermore, the group appeared frustrated at its inability to think and provide a safe space where vulnerabilities could be expressed and risks taken. For many of the women in the group, failing maternal function was rooted deeply in their experience, having endured the failure of primary carers to keep them safe, hold them in mind and foster development. This is frequently re-enacted within the prison institution. While prison may serve as a containing environment (Delshadian, 2003), the concrete responses of the prison system to trauma and acting-out behaviour can re-enact the experience of maternal failure (Rothwell, 2008).

Separation

This failure to keep in mind or protect those in its care was definitively re-enacted with the sudden and unexpected announcement that Holloway would close. The therapists were not present when the closure was announced. They heard the news through media announcements.

Figure 7.6

They were left shocked, angry and feeling worthless. This sense of being dispensable and undervalued may have mirrored the prisoners and staff around them. However, the therapists experienced a difficult personal response, feeling they had less entitlement to grieve over the loss. They felt excluded as "outsiders" providing a service which already had an "end date". Perhaps this feeling mirrored the state of "not belonging" that the group had struggled at times to contain. Nevertheless, grief was present. Within the group this was met with mixed responses as disbelief, indifference and jubilation gave way to shock and anger. It would however, take some time for the impact of the closure to be fully felt and processed by the group. At this time there were more immediate concerns, as the turbulence of adolescence threatened the group's survival.

Transition to adulthood

As the group resumed, the loss and grief that had emerged was exacerbated following a death in custody. This tragedy yet again brought up issues in the group around safety and care. Discussion focused on fear, powerlessness and terror. These conversations brought to the fore the disparity between group members' experiences of deprivation. One member of the group, Anna, recalled growing up in extreme poverty. Her image depicted her selling food on the side of the street and she spoke of the "not nice" men that came with it. While other group members found it difficult to relate to this level of material deprivation, they seemed to be able to identify with one another in terms of emotional deprivation. While rivalrous and dismissive of each other's experiences at times, it seemed that they had all had a sense of something lacking and their needs not being met in one way or another. Despite the group expressing anger and aggression, this seemed to have matured from the adolescent "tantrums" experienced earlier, to more powerful expressions relating to fear and what the closure of Holloway might mean to them as individuals. The closure was being digested and had come to be seen as a certainty. In this way, it seemed the group had progressed into adulthood and was coming to accept reality.

Mid-life crisis

As the months passed by the women settled back into the group. Relationships were tested and strengthened as images were made and acknowledged. With the end of Onyx on the horizon the therapists reminded the group that there were ten sessions left. This was met with immediate aggression, dismissal and denigration of the group as members announced that it was "useless" and they were leaving. This rejection and the women's difficulty in making sense of their feelings may have been influenced by their experiences of early trauma. It felt as if the group was experiencing a mid-life crisis amid a fear that the group would be destroyed. Mid-life crisis has been described as, "personal turmoil ... resulting from the realization of aging, physical declination or entrapment in certain roles ... sense of loneliness ... a time of frantic overload ... or change" (Wong, Awang and Jani, 2012: 805).

Within the group there seemed to be a denial of the end and a rejection of change. Perhaps it felt easier to reject the group than to experience its dispersing and accept the emptiness? Case (2000) describes the potential for symptoms to increase prior to a break due to powerful defences protecting against difficult feelings about the separation; and the likelihood for the therapist to be attacked at this time. While some members of the group seemed to have been able to manage the difficult process of separation and maturation, not all members seemed able to manage the finality of the approaching ending and disengaged through various means.

Anna seemed to be in a period of reflection during this time, with much of her work raising themes of identity and ageing. Having been trafficked to the United Kingdom and with an offence of controlling prostitution, Anna's early images had often taken the form of fairies and slender, Caucasian women which she told the group she was making for her son (Figure 7.7).

By the time the group hit its mid-life crisis Anna's artwork had changed and she was making images of women that related to her own identity (Figure 7.8). This was noted by other group members.

The images often depicted a solitary figure which highlighted her vulnerability as she spoke of her desire for a relationship. In this way Anna's artwork depicted these vulnerabilities and echoed her relationships with men throughout her life; providing food to them on the street, the sexual assaults that had come with this, providing women for male customers through her offence of controlling prostitution and onto her own experience of wanting to attract a man to take care of and love her. Anna seemed unable to manage the mid-life crisis of the group and the upcoming ending. She removed herself from the group, and while the therapists worked hard to re-engage Anna, she chose to attend other classes and individual therapy instead. Case asserts that patients in therapy,

> ... are vulnerable because as their defenses lessen they become more aware of feeling need and dependency and more in touch with the situation which has brought them into treatment. It is this which often leads to the breaking off of treatment.
>
> (Case, 2000: 12)

On visiting Anna to return her artwork, the therapists found her in a difficult place. The experience of having been unable to work towards a "good" ending with her felt like a failure (Edwards,

Figure 7.7

1997) and brought out mixed feelings of angry dismissal and sad disappointment in the therapists. They found joint supervision valuable in these situations as it enabled them to think together about the group in relation to their own feelings and allowed them to recognise their "individual differences". Dudley writes, "Dual processing by co-therapists is felt to be particularly useful when working with patients deemed 'difficult to treat' and stresses the importance of open dialogue in supervision in order to process what was happening in the group" (2001: 14–15). Anna seemed to have been unable to accept the difficult feelings in the group and had become more isolated, unable to connect with the group's feelings of rage and terror. Being unable to acknowledge these feelings within herself she had instead scapegoated the group and located the difficulties there.

Figure 7.8

During this time of change the therapists began to sit and work at the table together with the women, seemingly compelled to demonstrate a physical need to hold and contain the group (Bion, 1986). This "sitting together" had previously been intermittent and punctuated at times by the therapists sitting "in the background". At this point in the group's development the images created by the therapists during sessions seemed to relate to the anxieties which were present in the group, particularly survival and the fear of disintegration. The fragility of the group and the therapists' attempts to contain and hold it together were evident in the artwork. At the time the therapists believed their art making offered what Havsteen-Franklin and Camarena-Altamirano describe as, "an attuned visual response to the experience of being in the room with the patient ... amplifying or mirroring the feelings or gestures" (2015: 54). However, in supervision the therapists wondered if their art making was actually a demonstration of their own anxieties within the group, an amplification of which might have been experienced in the group as unsafe. Indeed, this acting out by the therapists might have left them less attuned to the needs of the group, less responsive and more likely to enact destructive unconscious behaviours (Brown, 2008). At this time it felt as if the therapists were merely surviving the attacks and projections ricocheting throughout the group. Perhaps their art-making was an attempt to contain their own anxieties.

The aging process

There was a shift in the group as some members removed themselves and new members joined. Maya, who had been with the group since the beginning, was transferred to another prison. She had arrived in the group on an Assessment, Care in Custody and Teamwork (ACCT) document, a risk-based audit used to monitor inmates where there is a concern about self-harm or suicide (Ministry of Justice. National Offender Management Service, 2011). Maya had initially made child-like, superficial images (Figure 7.9) that contradicted the terror and trauma she recounted.

However, Maya was no longer deemed a risk when her therapy came to an end. Some of her later images seemed more connected to the emotions she was expressing verbally and the feelings of emptiness she shared were reflected more coherently in her imagery (Figure 7.10).

In her final session Maya used materials to make a number of collages looking through a window. In one sat an old woman. Maya laughed that it was her in the future. Coming from a woman who had struggled with intense anxiety and suicidality, the image she created, illustrating a future in which she would grow old, felt hopeful. In another of Maya's images a person emerged from a brick wall and put their arms around another. Maya had often spoken about feeling safer within the prison and her fears surrounding release. Perhaps the brick wall in the image was the holding embrace that she had felt from Holloway and from Onyx.

Looking towards death

The group continued after Maya's departure. Vanya, who had attended the group for a number of months, had an index offence of fraud and was involved in a legal battle for access to her children. She had found it difficult to connect with the responsibility of her offence as well as her responsibility as a mother. Vanya had struggled to remain in the group after the most difficult and destructive session.

Figure 7.9

Figure 7.10

Her ambivalence, inconsistency and impulsivity had been a constant throughout the project but she managed to return to the group after some weeks.

In the initial sessions upon her return Vanya was on an ACCT document having started to self-harm. She was able to think about some of the difficulties she had experienced including losing group members. Much of the subsequent work focused on her own experiences of loss prior to joining the group and her process of forgiveness surrounding her separation from her children. Furthermore, it felt as though she was trying to forgive the therapists, possibly for ending the group. Towards the end Vanya became less vulnerable and was taken off an ACCT document. She made books and frames for pictures of her children and friends. In the final sessions Vanya brought prepared materials with her and worked frantically, trying to do as much as she could in the time available. She found it difficult to finish making art, voicing her feeling about the "unfairness" that the group had to end. Vanya made cardboard frames covered in swathes of tissue paper, as well as tissue paper bouquets of flowers. As she completed these she began laying them up against a stack of empty chairs to allow them to dry.

Following the session the therapists discussed how this action resembled laying wreaths at a memorial. As these "wreaths" and flowers had been stacked up at the base of the empty chairs they wondered about the previous group members who had left. Vanya seemed to be making painful unconscious feelings conscious and tangible. It felt as though Vanya was allowing herself to mourn the loss of the group and the death of the prison, the place that she considered home. Vanya's ability to re-engage with the group, after some difficulties, seemed to have allowed her to mature and to mourn what had been and was being lost. The therapist's wondered too if this interpretation was an illustration of their own unconscious response to the loss.

As landings shut down one by one and the prison emptied around them, broken furniture was thrown out into the prison grounds on to piles resembling mass graves. Group members diminished, and the prison disintegrated; there was no mistaking the ending was in sight.

> Ending a therapeutic relationship obliges both therapist and client to re-examine that relationship; to question its meaning and worth. The often painful feelings that emerge within the therapeutic

relationship as part of the ending process will, therefore, be experienced by both therapist and client.

(Edwards, 1997: 49)

This final stage of the group seemed to have taken on an element of old age, with members making memory books and frames for pictures to hold snapshots of past lives. It seemed as if the group, in its final decline, was looking for acceptance of imminent death. Time was running out and the women were looking back. Irma, a woman with memory problems who was waiting to be extradited, left an image with us when the group ended (Figure 7.11). She spoke of the quiet and her desire for peacefulness.

Conclusion

The therapists too had to accept the ending of the group into which they had put so much time and focus. Looking back, both therapists found that the group's maturation mirrored something of their distinct

Figure 7.11

individual journeys. They had to work with their feelings of loss for the group and for their own relationship.

The many women who had attended Onyx were from a number of diverse countries. There was not always a shared language in the room, but the art making seemed to make connection and communication possible. It may be useful to think about the specific function of art therapy with this particular client group as distinct from other forms of verbal therapy.

> The dependence on the use of the eyes and visual joint attention skills in art therapy distinguishes it from other forms of therapy...both patient and art therapist look together at the art object, in an attempt to share the feeling and possible meaning that its making may hold.
>
> (Isserow, 2008: 34, 41)

Isserow emphasises the importance of "looking together" at the artwork which may be an indicator into the usefulness of art therapy with a foreign national prison population.

Without a shared spoken language, verbal psychotherapeutic work was largely inaccessible to the foreign national women at Holloway. These women, facing uncertain futures, away from family and friends and without knowledge of the prison culture, were some of the most vulnerable of the prison population. The therapists believe the act of looking together at their images may have allowed the women to be seen in a world where they had often been forgotten.

ACKNOWLEDGEMENTS

The authors would like to thank the women who kindly gave their consent for their experiences to be included and for images of their artworks to be shared. Pseudonyms have been used throughout. They would also like to thank the Feminist Review Trust and Public Health Action Support Team for funding the Onyx Art Therapy Group project.

REFERENCES

Bion, W. R. (1959). Attacks on linking. *International Journal of Psycho-Analysis*, 40:308–315.

Bion, W. R. (1961). *Experiences in Groups*. London: Tavistock.

Bion, W. R. (1986). *Attention and Interpretation*. London: Karnac.
Brown, C. (2008). Very toxic – Handle with care. Some aspects of the maternal function in art therapy. *International Journal of Art Therapy: Formerly Inscape*, 13:13–24.
Canham, H. (2002). Group and gang states of mind. *Journal of Child Psychotherapy*, 28:113–127.
Case, C. (1999). Foreign images: Images of race and culture in therapy with children. In: J. Campbell, M. Liebmann, F. Brooks, J. Jones and C. Ward (eds), *Art Therapy, Race and Culture* (pp. 68–85). London: Jessica Kingsley.
Case, C. (2000). Santa's grotto an exploration of the Christmas break in therapy. *Inscape*, 5:11–18.
Corston, J. (2007). *The Corston Report*. London: Crown Publishing.
Delshadian, S. (2003). Playing with fire: Art therapy in a prison setting. *Psychoanalytic Psychotherapy*, 17:68–84.
Dudley, J. (2001). The co-therapist relationship a married couple? *Inscape*, 6:12–22.
Edwards, D. (1997). Endings. *Inscape*, 2:49–56.
Foucault, M. (1977). *Discipline and Punish: The Birth of the Prison*. London: Penguin.
Freud, S. (1915). The Unconscious. In J. Strachey (trans., ed.), *The Standard Edition of the Complete Psychological Works of Sigmund Freud*, vol. XIV (pp. 159–215). London: Hogarth Press.
Havsteen-Franklin, D. and Camarena Altamirano, J. (2015). Containing the uncontainable: Responsive art making in art therapy as a method to facilitate mentalization. *International Journal of Art Therapy: Formerly Inscape*, 20:54–65.
Isserow, J. (2008) Looking together: Joint attention in art therapy. *International Journal of Art Therapy*, 13(1): 34–42.
Ministry of Justice. National Offender Management Service. (2011). Quick-time learning bulletin: Assessment, care in custody & teamwork (ACCT). *National Safer Custody Managers & Learning Team Offender Safety, Rights & Responsibilities Group*, 9.
Prison Reform Trust. (2016). Bromley briefings prison factfile, Autumn 2016. Retrieved from www.prisonreformtrust.org.uk/Portals/0/Documents/Bromley%20Briefings/Autumn%202016%20Factfile.pdf (last accessed 4 March 2017).
Rothwell, K. (2008). What anger? Working with acting-out behaviour in a secure setting. In: M. Liebmann (ed.), *Art Therapy and Anger* (pp. 117–133). London: Jessica Kingsley.
Teasdale, C. (1995). Reforming zeal or fatal attraction: Why should art therapists work with violent offenders? *Inscape*, 2:2–9.

Winnicott, D. W. (1964). *The Child, the Family and the Outside World.* London: Penguin.

Winnicott, D. W. (1965). *The Maturational Processes and the Facilitating Environment.* London: The Hogarth Press.

Wong, L. P., Awang, H. and Jani, R. (2012). Midlife crisis perceptions, experiences, help-seeking, and needs among multi-ethnic Malaysian women. *Women and Health*, 52:804–819.

CHAPTER EIGHT

"I will never get out of here"

Therapeutic work with an Imprisonment for Public Protection prisoner caught up in the criminal justice system

Sabina Amiga

Introduction

This chapter is about the specific difficulties Imprisonment for Public Protection (IPP) prisoners share, including hopelessness and the near enough impossibility of proving they are no longer a risk to others. Jenny, whose case highlights these issues, has kindly given me permission to use some material from our work together; her name and details have been disguised. Jenny feels passionate about helping other IPP prisoners who are still incarcerated.

The prison officer on Jenny's landing looked at me with what I felt was a mixture of surprise and condescension when I asked to see Jenny for our first psychotherapy session. During the next few weeks I quickly learnt how little most people thought of her. Comments, some well-meant and usually accompanied by resigned shaking of heads, ranged from "you're wasting your time" to "she'll soon give up" to a devastating "she'll be here forever". But I wondered if this was what the judge had in mind when he gave Jenny an IPP sentence. Was the intention that she would stay in prison for the rest of her life? Jenny was only twenty years old when she was sentenced, and now the twenty-five months of her minimum tariff had long past and had turned into eight long years. Jenny was still in prison.

When the Criminal Justice Act of 2003 introduced Imprisonment for Public Protection (IPP), the objective was to shield the public from serious sexual and violent offenders in England and Wales. It was designed so those who posed a significant risk of causing serious harm to the public could be detained in prison until they no longer posed such a risk. The Ministry of Justice stated that

> Offenders sentenced to an IPP are set a minimum term (tariff) which they must spend in prison. After they have completed their tariff they can apply to the parole board for release. The parole board will release an offender only if it is satisfied that it is no longer necessary for the protection of the public for the offender to be confined. If offenders are given parole, they will be on supervised licence for at least ten years. If offenders are refused parole, they can only apply again after one year.
> (Ministry of Justice, 2011)

Meeting Jenny

I met Jenny in the association room of her landing. A glass door and narrow corridor separated us from where the prison officers were sitting and talking, glancing over to us from time to time. She came in and sat down in the chair furthest away from me, pulling her knees close to her chin, her white sunless arms protectively embracing her skinny legs. Jenny's casual clothes looked inappropriate for the time of the year. It was January and the prison notoriously under heated. To me her thin sleeveless shirt accentuated both her fragility and perhaps her wish to appear tough to the therapist who had come and might ask uncomfortable questions. It was her face, however, that bore the most striking armour. The dense layer of make-up and long fake eye lashes under darkly painted eye brows seemed too heavy for her small face and made it difficult to read her thoughts or emotions. While Jenny would later understand how she used her make-up to mask the self she was so desperate to hide from us, she could never bring herself "to face the world" without it.

Jenny was polite and surprisingly open as soon as we began to talk. This was her first "proper" attempt at therapy, she confirmed, and her declared goal was to "find out why I keep making stupid mistakes". Her choice of words betrayed the seriousness of her situation. For the first few sessions Jenny could not help but minimise any negativity in her life. Growing up was "a bit bad" rather than the shockingly chaotic and abusive reality of her childhood. The white-hot anger that would sometimes take hold of her she'd call "getting the hump", while the "stupid mistakes" were grave enough to have kept her in prison long past her tariff. It was her probation officer, Kate, who had referred her to psychotherapy in preparation for sitting parole. Kate was hoping that therapy would not just tick the box for the parole board as another course completed, but support Jenny in understanding her issues and make better choices in the future. I had worked with Kate in the past. She was a dedicated, if permanently overworked, probation officer who was always prepared to search for solutions to help her clients rather than treat them as cases that needed to be shifted from her desk. However, in her referral, Kate had left me in no doubt that to achieve lasting improvements in Jenny's behaviour would take great effort.

> Jenny: "I didn't really want to start therapy but it was either this or going to a different prison. So I thought I'd give it a try but I was petrified. I didn't want anyone to know my life, to write it down in one of those reports that they keep writing about me and are never true. I was worried I'd be misunderstood and that what I'd say would be used against me."

Cycles of offending

Jenny spoke quietly and matter-of-fact, with little trace of emotion in her voice. Yet, talking about her family was hard for her; something she had never done before. She assured me that she was determined to "give it a real go" at therapy, having finally realised that if she did not find a way to convince the parole board of having changed, she might "stay in prison forever". Jenny came from a notorious crime family. Her father had been in and out of jail before he was killed during a robbery when Jenny was five years old. Her mother, as well as her three children, became well-known to police and social services for their drug and alcohol abuse and their anti-social behaviour. Giving a little joyless smile and looking coyly at me to ascertain my reaction, Jenny disclosed that their photos would be displayed in convenience stores where she and her family would regularly shoplift. Bottles of alcohol would be brazenly taken and anyone trying to intervene would be physically fought. From an early age, Jenny had opposed authority figures and "their petty rules". Teachers, policemen, social workers and now prison officers, would be verbally, sometimes violently, attacked. It was for an assault on a security guard that she received the IPP. Jenny had hit him and bitten him during her arrest. The judge expressed his "disgust" and remarked that he was "fed up" with her behaviour and therefore sentenced her indefinitely until she could prove she had become a "law-abiding" person.

Originally, the government estimated that IPP would lead to 900 extra offenders entering the prison system but IPP numbers grew rapidly, with many in jail well past their minimum terms. It soon became apparent that the government had not been clear in setting out sentencing criteria for judges and that resources to ensure rehabilitation had not been effective enough. They were designed to protect the public from serious offenders but have been used far more widely than intended, with some issued to offenders who have committed low level crimes with tariffs as short as two years. IPPs have proved difficult to understand and leave victims and their families uncertain about how and when an offender will be released. IPPs lead to inconsistent sentencing. They have been given to some offenders, while others who have committed similar crimes have served fixed sentences (Prison Reform Trust, 2014).

First, she tried to shrug off the judge's words as well as his IPP sentencing, unable to comprehend the gravity and consequences. Until this point Jenny had followed the same destructive path her entire family had taken. She had spent most of her young life in a mad dance around institutions from the age of twelve, when her mother had declared she "could not handle" her anymore and Jenny had gone onto care. She passed from care homes to secure children's homes and, via young offender institutions, to her first adult prison. These were interrupted by short visits at home where she would quickly fall back into the spiral of drink and drugs, theft, assault and arrest. During her incarcerations, Jenny would present as rebellious and belligerent, with a quick wit and even quicker tongue. She would quickly assume the role of leader and speak out for others as if compelled to intervene, constantly getting herself "into trouble" with officers. As a teenager, Jenny had revelled in her reputation as uncontrollable and disobedient and she brought this same attitude to her latest prison term. But an IPP sentence is very different. Her tariff came and went and so did many parole hearings. By the time Jenny had turned twenty eight and we had begun working together, her defiance had withered to a few outbursts that officers could easily identify as a façade to hide the terror of staying indefinitely in prison.

By 2012 it had become apparent that IPP sentences kept thousands of men and women in prison cells long after they have served the portion of their sentences deemed by the judges to be sufficient for their punishment. They could regain their freedom only by satisfying a risk-averse parole board and predictably, the requirement to prove a future has set IPP prisoners an almost impossible task, and only a tiny percentage of IPP prisoners had been released by then, even though in many cases their original offences have been relatively minor – as their often short minimum sentences have shown. Described by the Prison Reform Trust as "Kafkaesque", IPP sentences were abolished in 2012 by then justice secretary Ken Clarke, who called them a "stain" on the criminal justice system. He said that it was "almost impossible" for a prisoner to prove that he was no longer a risk to the public. IPP was scrapped but not retrospectively, with more than 6000 existing IPP prisoners remaining on this sentence.

(Guardian, 2016)

The therapeutic relationship

When we started therapy together, little did either of us know that our work would stretch from an anticipated few months to more than two years as the date of her parole hearing would constantly, through no fault of hers, be pushed back.

Jenny: "And worst of all, my family did not believe it was out of my hands, that I must have done something bad 'cause they wouldn't let me sit parole; nobody understands how IPP works."

Like Jenny, I felt condemned to wait powerlessly until the wheels of bureaucracy finally began to spin in her direction. "Misinformation and misunderstandings can contribute to an overwhelming sense of confusion and desperation, and a feeling that IPP prisoners were 'left in the dark' which could cause frustration to them and members of their families" (Sainsbury Centre for Mental Health, 2008). While I tried to keep strict boundaries as one of the cornerstones of forensic psychotherapy, my mounting frustration with the slow-moving justice system became somewhat entangled with Jenny's own anger towards authority. At times, I struggled with the unfairness of it all: hadn't Jenny been penalised enough? I wondered how many more years of her young life she would have to waste in prison in order to feed society's hunger for punishment. Just as I needed the help of my supervision group to work through my own conflicting feelings, Jenny used our sessions to understand and learn to contain the toxic mixture of sadness and aggression that kept disturbing her mind and had been ruining her life.

> *Jenny: "What I liked about therapy was that I could talk about anything. I was beginning to understand myself better and where I was going wrong."*

Life in prison

The reality of day-to-day life for an IPP prisoner soon became clear to me. Jenny shared with other women the crushing monotony of indistinguishable meals, often mindless activities and many hours spent locked in small cells thick with cigarette smoke and simmering tension between the women. What set her and other IPP prisoners apart was the absolute uncertainty of their future. Working towards the parole hearing proved difficult, as dates vanished as quickly as they were set, frequently leaving Jenny utterly deflated. It enforced her contempt of anything and anyone in authority as "they don't give a shit about me" and substantiated her resigned belief that whatever she tried to improve, her situation would come to nothing. Her frustration when fused with despair could easily rattle her resolve "to stay out of trouble" after yet another setback. This would then need careful examination and calming words during sessions where I tried to help Jenny contain her emotions when they threatened to run away with her. Securely attached children acquire affect regulation through attuned parenting early on (Bowlby, 1980). This had been missing in Jenny's early life. Therapy offered the opportunity to become aware of her childhood experiences and how she was acting these out through offending. Understanding those links might help her to regulate and tolerate painful and angry feelings that might otherwise have been acted out or defended against by misuse of drugs and alcohol; in turn driving her offending.

These changes take time, but Jenny made good progress during those months of enforced waiting and wretched hopes. Concentrating on the unpredictable nature of the parole process, however, seemed to give her some reprieve from the real monster in the room: what if the parole board once again found against her? It was only on a few occasions that Jenny shared with me the complete hopelessness she felt; "I'll never get out of here", she'd say to me.

Over four years since the abolition of IPP sentencing, there are still over 4,000 people in prison serving this discredited sentence, unsure when or if they will ever be released. Four out of every five are still stuck behind bars despite having served their minimum term, no longer in prison for what they have done, but for what they might do. Peter Clarke, Chief Inspector of Prisons warned:

> decisive action must be taken by the Justice Secretary to reduce the number of prisoners with a sentence of imprisonment for public protection (IPP) who are still in prison years after the end of their tariff. The impact on individuals who have, to all effects and purposes, served their sentences but don't have any scheduled date of release is devastating.
>
> (Converse Prison News, 2016).

Working in therapy

However difficult her situation, Jenny seemed to maintain her respect for the therapy. She never missed a session in all those months. Intelligent and curious, she became intrigued by the way her neglectful and abusive early life experiences and the links to her current difficulties slowly unravelled. She courageously began to ask questions she had never dared asking before. Her resistance to seeing her family criticised was evident at the beginning of therapy. Like so many women who have experienced similarly deprived and traumatic backgrounds, she clung to the idea of an ideal parent: anything less was too painful to contemplate. But as a measure of the trust building between us, she allowed me insights into the violence she had witnessed. She tentatively spoke of the devastating neglect she had suffered as a child growing up in chaos and crime, where she – still herself a child – had to assume the role of parent. Jenny described looking after her younger siblings as well as her mother whenever she was incapacitated by alcohol and drugs.

The only way Jenny could make sense of her surroundings was to follow her family's mantra of "us versus them" onto the path of violence. In doing so she unconsciously fulfilled the prediction so often heard by her that "you're just like your mother and you'll end up like her". Just as her family had done, Jenny considered anyone outside of her immediate circle, particularly people in authority, "enemies" who would carry all her ill feelings and could therefore be despised and dehumanised. Her black-and-white thinking was all-pervasive at the beginning of therapy and needed to be challenged and replaced by a more thoughtful approach.

It has been suggested in the literature for many years that someone like Jenny may acquire this kind of disorganised attachment style through unpredictable and often violent parenting. Individuals who have suffered in this way may have an under-developed ability to understand and represent the states of their own and other people's minds; characterised as an inability to "mentalise" (Fonagy, Gergely, Jurist and Target, 2002). In our sessions we used examples of her every-day interactions to enhance her "mentalising" skills in an attempt to help her understand how she could be perceived as well as contemplate more than one aspect of what could be in the mind of the other. Jenny had always routinely dismissed staff as hostile and being "always against" her and would assume the worst intentions with her automatic belief that "I know exactly what they are thinking". As therapy progressed, Jenny began instead to examine alternative scenarios: What if the officer had her best interest in mind when he tried to calm her down? Maybe the unfriendly face of the nurse had nothing to do with Jenny but was due to some problems at home?

In order to consider the other person's state of mind, we had to work on slowing Jenny's rigid thinking down, giving her time to deliberate rather than jump to conclusions and lash out. Thus, we used the concept of "mentalisation" as a means of protection against interpersonal violence. Jenny surprised herself by becoming more curious about others. Officers she used to detest and see merely as "screws" became individuals with names and histories. This development had the pleasant side-effect of staff feeling much warmer and more protective towards Jenny.

At the heart of forensic psychotherapy is the consideration of the index offence. All incidents of violence have a meaning and may represent an attempt to avoid something else too painful to face directly (Bartlett and McGauley, 2010). While Jenny felt ashamed of hurting the security guard who had tried to stop her from shoplifting, remorse alone could not make sense of what had happened. In our sessions we tried to understand what drove Jenny to act violently. As she became more aware of the links between her early life experiences and acting these out through offending, Jenny could see how her victim might have represented despised authority, as well as the men in her life who had disappointed and abused her. Half his size, Jenny stood no chance against the security guard physically, yet she leapt on his back, punching and biting him just as an enraged child might do.

In my own mind, I could not help but suspect that the social and emotional context of her offence had been lost to the sentencing judge. It seemed to me that instead of taking her circumstances into account, his remarks may have been influenced by society's unconscious bias against women. As adults, we are generally more tolerant of aggression in boys than in girls: nice girls don't hit and they certainly don't bite. If a woman breaks away from the female role Western society has stereotyped her in, undesirable behaviour may be controlled by labelling her as deviant or evil. She may even be more promptly regarded as mentally ill (Lemma, 1999). The punishment for Jenny's socially unacceptable and "disgusting" act was swift and severe: an indeterminate sentence to keep her away from the outside world for as long as possible. Nevertheless, despite the real possibility of gender bias motivating sentencing, it was important that I think about the intense emotional response I was experiencing. My previous professional work as a solicitor and my therapeutic relationship with Jenny threatened to become entwined and could potentially draw me into an unhelpful collusion with Jenny against a judge – the face of authority – that I might not be fully conscious of. Transference feelings between the therapist and the patient can be powerful and need to be carefully disentangled where necessary. I had to be comfortable that my thoughts were my own; not an unconscious presentation of Jenny's fear and disdain of authority or my own unconscious re-enactment of Jenny's "family" berating those who acted "against" them.

Apart from the long wait for a parole hearing, Jenny struggled most with the persistent and intense scrutiny she felt she was under. This fed her sometimes paranoid mistrust of others and was complicated by the confusion and uncertainty of the system she was immersed in; another unwelcome aspect of being an IPP prisoner. Anything remotely negative about her behaviour could be noted and put into writing. This might then be included in prison reports that would be permanently recycled. This feeling of paranoia was compounded by the reality that the prison management and probation officers hold great power.

Jenny: "I was stressed all the time because I was trying to be good but I was going nowhere. My mind's been racing. They've got us in a corner. I often felt like an animal that had to jump through hoops. Enough was never enough."

As testament to her improved relationship to the officers on her landing, their comments on Jenny's conduct became less negative and for the first time in her long prison sentence she was given praise for helping staff. Her behaviour at least was under her own control. What made her situation more precarious was prison "intel". This was information routinely collected by the prison intelligence unit and could come from any source including other prisoners who may have held a grudge against Jenny. In order to escape the constant surveillance – perceived or real – Jenny withdrew more and more from social interactions and hardly left her landing. I could not help but be reminded of Bentham's cruel eighteenth-century idea of the panopticon. This was a concept of institutional architecture where inmates could be observed at all times without knowing if they were being watched or not. This would render the inmate to a state of conscious and permanent visibility to assure the automatic functioning of power: one is totally seen without ever seeing (Foucault, 1977).

> Government statistics show that levels of mental distress are higher among IPP prisoners than among either the general prison population or prisoners serving life sentences. More than half of IPP prisoners have problems with "emotional wellbeing" compared with two-fifths of life prisoners and one-third of all prisoners.
> (Sainsbury Centre for Mental Health, 2008)

Time passing

Seasons passed without Jenny noticing as she would refuse to join others on outdoor activities. With no eye for the change in nature beyond her small cell window, she dressed in the same clothes come winter or summer. Jenny had given up her cherished job as peer supporter and eventually spent most days in her room, becoming restless and irritable, yet unable to express her frustration and fears other than the occasional confiding in friends or her sessions with me. Her description of "having to walk on eggshells" highlighted the near-impossibility for her to conform in such a pressure-cooker environment. It seemed the slightest transgression – such as answering back to an officer – could potentially jeopardise a positive outcome in her parole hearing. In those long months waiting for a definite date, I believe it was her rebellious streak – so destructive in the past – that kept her from giving up. But I wondered for how much longer. I had seen other IPP prisoners falling into depression, self-harming or resorting to violence.

> Insecurity is a part of the psychology of prisoners, imposed by the uncertainties of the prison environment ... The deprivation of personal responsibility leads to vulnerability, depression and a reduced ability or will to communicate. These feelings are aggravated by the uncertain length of custody for people on remand and serving indeterminate sentences.
> (Prison Reform Trust, 2010)

Re-enactments

Interpreting her self-imposed isolation as a re-enactment of her family's own abrupt split from community and friends some twenty years previously, I worried about the effect it had on her mental well-being as well as on the progress Jenny had made in therapy. I felt myself getting pulled further into her fight for release. That sentiment was not exceptional. Supporting our patients beyond the strict boundaries of a fifty minute session has always been part of the philosophy that some psychotherapists at HMP Holloway had sought to implement. In addition to writing reports for the parole board or sitting in meetings with other prison services, we would try to co-ordinate with internal and external organisations to help with housing, employment or childcare issues and where appropriate, offer post-release therapy "through-the-gate". In Jenny's case, I felt compelled to help make the next parole hearing her last. I made this decision while being conscious that my stance could be perceived as a re-enactment of Jenny's own fight against authority. I was therefore, mindful that my wish to stand up for justice in general and Jenny in particular might stretch beyond our well established therapeutic relationship. As such I had to make sure that I would model a good enough parent – encouraging and fair and enforcing her positive potential – rather than become a parent like figure who would fight the world indiscriminately just as her mother had.

The long and thorny road to sit parole felt to me at times like falling down a rabbit hole and landing feet first in a kind of topsy-turvy world where my trust in justice was severely tested. When I attended a multi-agency public protection arrangements (MAPPA) meeting to give evidence of Jenny's improved psychological understanding, I became aware of how weighted the process can be against offenders. Criminal actions and behavioural misconduct, however far in the past, were given priority in the panel's thinking over my own statement or the thoughtful review offered by Jenny's probation officer supporting release. Indeed the current prison probation officer's opinion was given less attention than the report based on previous data by Jenny's outside probation officer. This individual had met Jenny only once before, yet stated that Jenny should undertake a lengthy course only available in a different prison. A move Jenny had refused.

> Jenny: "She doesn't know me at all but my life depends on her. They will always try to move the goal posts but if I don't get out now, I never will."

I argued that the progress she had made during her one-to-one treatment in psychotherapy would outweigh the benefits of the proposed course. However, the thought I had that the course might be used to defer release by a risk-adverse parole board, I kept to myself. Sadly, the obvious peculiarity of Jenny's situation – that she was still in prison long after her tariff had expired for an IPP prison sentence that had since been abolished – was largely ignored in all the meetings I had with government bodies discussing Jenny's case.

Nevertheless, against the odds and following further setbacks, Jenny remained hopeful but acutely aware of the steep mountain she was to climb in order to convince the justice system that she had changed considerably and ceased to pose a risk to others. When the date of the oral hearing finally arrived, Jenny presented herself as calm and composed, her pale face made up into an impenetrable mask. She gave me a faint smile before she sat down to turn to the parole board. It was her day and she knew she had to make it count.

Epilogue

More than ten years after her conviction and eight years after the tariff of twenty-five months had expired, the parole board concluded that Jenny should be released. This was not unconditional. She was to be held for an indeterminate length of time at an approved hostel, ostensibly to help her ease back into life "on the outside". However, the sudden loss of her support system at HMP Holloway combined with the prospect of yet another unspecified period of confinement and surveillance triggered intense anxiety and finally proved too much for Jenny. Two weeks after I visited her at the hostel where she appeared erratic and agitated but nonetheless resolved "to make it", Jenny was recalled back to prison. As an enduring legacy of the IPP sentence, Jenny remains on licence indefinitely. She was found in violation of one of her licence conditions when she took a "legal high" to help her, she explained, "escape a bit". It seems there is no escape for Jenny. She is now incarcerated in an unfamiliar prison, HMP Holloway having closed in the interim.

Any institution that deprives individuals of their liberty, however necessary, operates with a degree of dysfunction and disturbance. HMP Holloway, accommodating over five hundred often neglected and vulnerable women, was no exception. Though intended as punishment for the offences these women had committed, for years it provided a more consistent and containing home than some prisoners had ever experienced in the community. For many it became a home that encompassed familiar faces, officers and therapists that offered help and support. With its closure, any further work between Jenny and myself became impossible. We both now live with the disappointment of what could have been but never was: a real chance.

REFERENCES

Bartlett, A. and McGauley, G. (eds) (2010). *Forensic Mental Health: Concepts, Systems, and Practice.* New York: Oxford University Press.

Bowlby, J. (1980). *A Secure Base.* London: Routledge.

Converse Prison News (2016). Justice secretary must bring down number of prisoners sentenced for public protection still in jail years after tariff, says chief inspector. *Converse Prison News,* November. http://converseprisonnews.com/category/ipp-lifer-sentences/

Fonagy, P., Gergely, G., Jurist, E. L., Target, M. (2002). *Affect Regulation, Mentalization and the Development of the Self.* New York: Other Press.

Foucault, M. (1977). Discipline and punish, panopticism. In A. Sheridan (ed.), *Discipline and Punish: The Birth of the Prison* (pp.195–228). New York: Vintage Books.

Guardian. (2016). Ken Clarke: "absurd" that defunct prison scheme still keeps people in jail. *The Guardian,* 30 May. www.theguardian.com/society/2016/may/30/absurd-defunct-prison-scheme-ken-clarke-james-ward-jail-mental-health

Lemma, A. (1999). *Introduction to Psychopathology.* London: Sage Publications.

Ministry of Justice. (2011). IPP factsheet. www.justice.gov.uk/downloads/legislation/bills-acts/legal-aid-sentencing/ipp-factsheet.pdf

Prison Reform Trust. (2010). Prisons can seriously damage your mental health. www.prisonreformtrust.org.uk/uploads/documents/Mentalhealthsmall.pdf

Prison Reform Trust. (18 March 2014). Imprisonment for public protection is a stain on our justice system. www.prisonreformtrust.org.uk/PressPolicy/News/vw/1/ItemID/208

Sainsbury Centre for Mental Health. (2008). *In the Dark: The Mental Health Implications of Imprisonment for Public Protection*. London: Sainsbury Centre for Mental Health.

CHAPTER NINE

"I could do it on my eyelashes"

Holding the unthinkable for the unthinking patient

Frances Maclennan and Catherine McCoy

Introduction

There are two central principles of forensic therapeutic work regarded as essential: the index offence and the team.

> The more patients empty their minds of painful memories, the more staff member's minds and case notes are filled with them. Ultimately, the combined burden of remembering and the unrelenting pressure from patients to forget affects staff members and teams
>
> (John Gordon in Welldon, 2011: 155)

The fragmented patient and the splits within their mind can be projected into the teams and systems that they are held within. These splits are important communications. There is a real need for the team to make time and space to reflect upon such a dynamic in order to make sense of its meaning. At HMP Holloway, many of the women incarcerated had suffered the unthinkable, and had consequently committed unthinking actions. Painful early experiences of abuse and neglect had destroyed the very capacity to think. Distrust, suspicion and fear pervaded the minds of many within the prison.

Contemplating the unthinkable parts of other minds can be difficult, partly because it is frightening to consider the dark potential of the mind, but also because most of us wish to hide these parts of ourselves from the world. Offenders have rarely been given the opportunity to explore either their internal or external worlds. The theory of "mentalization", posits that a person's sense of self develops by observing oneself being perceived by others as thinking or feeling. Failures of parental responsiveness cause a failure in the capacity to "mentalize" and thus an unstable and incoherent sense of self (Bateman and Fonagy, 2004).

Behind the high brick walls of HMP Holloway and the barbed wire fences above them, there were endless limitations, rules, rigid systems; even rats. Prisons are suspicious and frightening places. They do however, simultaneously provide some women with a rare opportunity; containment. Many women incarcerated here had never experienced feeling secure or protected from sexual, physical and emotional abuse. Rarely had any of the women who came into Holloway been able to explore their experiences in a safe place. Inevitably coming to prison marked the first time their acts of violence or criminality had been thought about meaningfully. At times, the rigidity of the system within the walls of HMP Holloway had the effect of creating a predictable and therefore more manageable environment for some of the women who lived there. The prison provided a rare opportunity for some women to think, and for the first time for many, to be thought about. Nevertheless, prisons can be difficult places to develop strong teams and good working relationships. Paranoia and fear often pervade through the prison walls and staff can be understandably frightened.

In presenting "Queen Lizzie", the name this woman gave herself, we hope to illustrate how these two fundamental principles of forensic therapy – looking for meaning and working collaboratively – come together to hold both the team and the patient through the difficult process of treatment. We will discuss how the institution and the clinicians were able at times to think about our patient and to tolerate her projections. We will focus on how difficult it seemed for this woman to think about her offence of fraud, and how this penetrated every part of her mind and body and was alive in every aspect of her treatment.

In this chapter, we want to reflect on how prison made it possible to think together about a person who had perhaps, never been thought about before.

Queen Lizzie

Lizzie was a 42-year-old black woman, born and brought up in the UK. She stood out against the rest of the prison population with her statuesque figure. She was always well presented, dressed fashionably, her hair neatly braided. She moved gracefully and with confidence through the prison corridors, and yet, at my first meeting with her, she sat, swinging her feet, her finger in her mouth, akin to a small, shy 6-year-old.

Lizzie grew up in Manchester and had three siblings, an older brother and sister and one younger brother. Like so many women at HMP Holloway, criminality had pervaded her family and two of her siblings were currently serving sentences in prison. Lizzie claimed that her mother had been given a one way ticket back to Brazil from her husband when Lizzie was just eleven years old. Soon after her mother's departure, Lizzie was sent away to boarding school and they never saw each other again.

As an adult, Lizzie had met her long term partner when she was working as a model. He was a successful athlete and upon early retirement he and Lizzie started a family business in Spain. They had one son, now a teenager, who had followed in her steps as a model.

Lizzie had been in and out of HMP Holloway five times over the years. For the most part, she had been charged and found guilty of shoplifting. Her method would be to steal an item, then return it in order to claim the cash refund. On this occasion, she was serving a three-year sentence for breaching an Anti-Social Behavioural Order (ASBO). Lizzie had knocked on the doors of vulnerable old people and told them a story of desperation and need. With some additional pressure on her victims, she would then take their money and spend it on heroin and crack. Lizzie didn't think; she was motivated by using drugs. She had not been thought about as a child and as an adult had been unable to consider her own destructive actions. Lizzie found people were unreliable. She trusted drugs more than relationships as she knew exactly what she would get from them. Lizzie had caused immense pain and fear to her victims. Her own childhood experience of maternal pain and rejection had been repeated in her own adulthood. Just as she had been abandoned by her mother, she abandoned her own son, having spent a total of eight years in prison. The cyclical pattern of familial re-enactment was once again playing out.

Lizzie in the prison

Lizzie was referred to the psychological therapies team by the prison GP. She had presented to them with severe type 1 diabetes and her health was of significant concern. Managing her diabetes within the prison environment had become increasingly difficult as she had a serious eating disorder. Most days Lizzie would binge on sweets and fizzy drinks. She would then make herself sick which in turn would cause her blood sugars to drop dramatically. She would regularly have hypo attacks in which she would vomit, go dizzy, fall to the ground and be unable to move. The prison staff were extremely concerned about Lizzie. If diabetes is not carefully managed the resulting high glucose can wreak havoc on nearly every organ system in the body; resulting in blindness, kidney failure and amputation. Lizzie had recently had eye surgery and her hands were in such a poor state that the team at times thought that she might have to have her right hand removed. However, the real concern was that she might die in prison due to her poor diet and subsequent diabetic attacks. Lizzie's levels of self-harm had become increasingly repetitive and anxiety provoking to the Holloway prison medical team. Emergency services were regularly called into the prison to attend to her needs. Although Lizzie had been told of the seriousness of her condition, she could not or would not regulate her eating and thus was placing herself in grave danger.

Lizzie's referral to psychological therapies was therefore driven by very real anxieties about her fragile health; anxieties which by now had penetrated the prison staff. Her self-harm was entirely regulating her relationships with the prison and the people within it. Her attack on her body also felt like an attack on the health professionals around her. Lizzie was referred to the psychological therapies team for some support around helping her to manage her eating disorder, her chaotic behaviour and to help the primary care service assist her to manage her diabetes.

Nursing staff and the GPs seemed to struggle with their reproving responses to Lizzie. The view of the GPs was that Lizzie presented as "a very risky patient" who was playing with life and death. The team appeared to interpret her behaviour of vomiting as a woman who was both "manipulative and greedy". She took much time from health services and demanded high levels of "care" through a behaviour that was interpreted as entirely within her control. Her capacity to cause mayhem on the landings and to direct the flow of resources to herself was seen as "unfair" and as depriving other more needy patients of their right to treatment. The narrative both inside and outside of the prison of "who gets what" was of ongoing concern and subjugated many other narratives that might have been more constructive.

Officers had a similar view; Lizzie to them represented a well-known story. A familiar woman who abused drugs and whose behaviour patterns had become dominated by the need to gain resources in order to get those drugs. The lengths Lizzie went to in the community to get money for heroin were mirrored within the prison walls by the dramatic scenes she was prepared to make in order to "gain attention". Lizzie's method of "getting" was experienced by many as extremely abusive; much like her method of theft in the community. Her attack on her own body through her violent use of food was experienced by some as an attack upon the "caring" system around her.

By the time the referral to psychological therapies came to us, the prison was reeling from the sudden and unexpected closure announcement and Lizzie's situation had further deteriorated; concerns were high. Within Holloway, it was often the case that the more anxiety around a patient, the more binary and rigid our thinking became around that patient. Indeed, it appeared to us, that the responses to Lizzie were "breaking her up" rather than making sense of her as a whole individual. The podiatrist was concerned with her foot, the doctor with her insulin levels, nurses with the purge, she with the binge, the officers with controlling her behaviour on the landings and the governors with getting her safely moved to another prison. Lizzie was seen as a "troublemaker" and as "extremely manipulative". While the teams worked hard to keep her alive, her control on the systems around her was causing frustration and anger.

The referral we received was short and lacked detail: "This woman is bulimic, probably depressed, struggles with relationships. She has diabetes and her issues around eating are causing major difficulties." As HMP Holloway prepared to close, the therapeutic options were narrowing. Long term psychotherapy was unlikely. Furthermore, rarely would such a routine and familiar referral end up on the psychotherapist's caseload, partly because such cases were often in the prison for short sentences.

Within our work, understanding the internal world of the patient is crucial. Our task within the prison was to think about the patient's patterns of behaviour, to gently understand the complex layers that had built up over years and to seek meaning in the offences that brought them to the prison. With Lizzie, we aimed to explore the interpersonal contexts she had lived within and the responses she invoked through this complex myriad of interactions.

Lizzie in the group

With so few options available, Lizzie was referred to a weekly group that provided a first step into thinking about the internal world. It was informed by cognitive behavioural principles and its task was to encourage and support women to think about and better understand their thoughts, feelings and behaviours. Over the years this group had gained a certain richness. It provided a consistent and contained space for many women to come and think and reflect with others. Prison staff trusted the group and would refer complex and vulnerable women to us. It was often the first place to refer women who were considered unable to tolerate the intensity of individual work. Colleagues from different therapeutic paradigms began to regard the group as useful and appropriate. Within the confines of the prison, it was seen as a safe space for many women to think and to be thought about.

The group also functioned as an assessment for further treatments and as a short term therapeutic intervention for women who were likely to be transferred out of the prison quickly. Women could come to the group for a period of up to eight weeks. Following this, they might be referred into individual work or other therapeutic groups within the prison. At the time of Lizzie's referral there were five other women in the group. Much of the focus had been about the "ending" of Holloway and we had spent time reflecting upon other difficult endings that group members had experienced. The membership felt well established and as the closure of Holloway drew closer, an emotional openness had been with the group for some time. We wondered if the group might provide an opportunity for Lizzie to reflect upon her current situation. It seemed to us that she was communicating something profound through her behaviour. She appeared to be abusing and attacking herself through her eating. In the presence of a receptive mind, we wondered if she might be able to reflect on where she was, who she was and what she might hope for in the future. The group might offer her a place to think about the physical and how it connects to the mind.

Lizzie didn't fit the picture of the women who had been presented to us in the referral meeting: "critical", "unfit" or in "danger of losing her life". Instead, in came a tall, slim, neat and well-dressed woman who skipped into the room, in an almost childlike manner. She took to her chair, tucked her hair neatly behind her ears, and while fluttering her eyelashes announced to the room "I am Queen Elizabeth". She seemed outwardly confident; not a woman who had just had an operation to save her sight and was at risk of losing her hand through amputation. Lizzie did not share any of the details of her index offence with the group. She giggled and said she was caught "shoplifting for glamorous goodies". Instead, she shared stories of a sun soaked Mediterranean life. She spoke of eating good food, of parties, of money and of having "things". Lizzie spoke of her model son who had just secured a lucrative contract with a high-end cosmetic company and a partner who cared for and loved her. It became common in the group for her to talk about how she was "different from the other girls in prison". She felt others were "jealous of me" because she had money and because of how she looked. Her narrative was often seductive and she spoke of her wealthy brothers and sisters often sending her expensive labelled clothing into the prison, a place where poverty and disadvantage was, of course, rife. Lizzie presented a side of herself that was "powerful". She spoke endlessly about wealth, money, love, beauty and fashion. We wondered how this must feel for some of the other women in the group; how it left them feeling as Lizzie filled the room with her glitzy stories. At that time, we had some particularly vulnerable women in the group, all of whom had at some point been addicted to heroin and who had shared with the group the horrors of their experiences and the agony of awaking from it surrounded by the loss and pain they had brought about. Lizzie, it seemed, was unable to show any compassion.

In the group, Lizzie's presentation appeared contradictory and confusing. We often found ourselves wondering if she was behaving "fraudulently", presenting herself as privileged royalty in contrast to the reality of her emotionally deprived experience. We were confused by the conflicting stories she told. She described living in sun drenched bliss surrounded by people who loved her and were successful and beautiful, while the reports we had read detailed desperate drug addiction, fraud and a long history of stealing from the vulnerable and elderly. Lizzie seemed to make the best of what she had but if you looked closer her clothes were not designer, her hair tidy but not unusual, and although striking, she wasn't beautiful. We found we did not know who we were working with at all. Beneath the surface, this well-presented woman was slowly killing herself. We wondered if we were working with a "false self" (Winnicott, [1960]1987).

In fact, Lizzie made us think of the three card trickster; the oldest of card frauds. Otherwise known as "find the lady", it is impossible to win. In her offences, Lizzie had moved money around various bank accounts, in her own scheming game of hide and seek. We wondered whether Lizzie was moving reality around in her own mind and the minds of others. She seemed unable to hold anything solid in one place, just as she was unable to hold onto the food inside her. Lizzie seemed to be playing a role; she became the liar, the trickster, the fraudster. We wondered what she was communicating to us. At times we felt as if this fiction of Lizzie's was in some way protecting her and those around her, including us, from the loss and pain of her reality. We wondered if the group could support Lizzie in moving from the idealized fantasy in her own mind to exploring an alternative, more realistic narrative.

It became clear that Lizzie's capacity for relationships and friendships was limited. Rarely did we see her appear curious or inquisitive about others. Unless the subject was her, she would lean backwards in her chair and her eyes would half close. If she disagreed she would roll her eyes and laugh. Lizzie appeared to divide and rule, creating a split between those that could be her friend and those who could not. With a flutter of her eyelashes, she surveyed her dominion. Nevertheless, Lizzie was generous in the currency of physical objects. There seemed to be an unspoken promise that as a loyal subject of Queen Elizabeth, you would be repaid with access to the finer things of prison life; sweets, cigarettes and protection. We were curious about why Lizzie wanted allies and wondered who she wanted to be "kept safe" from. Meanwhile, Lizzie secured her status as privileged, special, and the "queen" of the group. Interestingly, her powerful capacity to take control of her surroundings was mirrored within the wider institution. Lizzie had fostered enough anxiety within the prison that she received special meals, regular nursing visits, weekly groups, weekly sessions with a psychiatrist and weekly individual sessions with a psychotherapist. This was her realm and she ruled.

Lizzie often dominated the group with her stories, loud laughter, opinions and her tears; although one group member pointed out "there are no actual tears there". The discussion would often focus on Lizzie, and the group struggled to pull back from this focus. One week Lizzie shared a story with the group about being with her partner in Spain. It had been a beautiful day and they had been to the beach. They returned to the bar, and Lizzie picked a fight with him. On this occasion, she appeared curious and was interested as to *why* she wanted to destroy something that had been good. She shared that this was a common experience for her.

Lizzie in the minds of the therapists

In our minds, Lizzie's destructive capacities were frightening to her. Whether real or imagined, in her mind she had been abandoned by her mother and father. Her early childhood had been chaotic and her parents had been unable to contain the family. She told the group that her father was unable to give her time or emotional support, but was able to buy her gifts. She compared him to her own wealthy husband who had been able to communicate only through material objects. At this time she seemed unable to name, think about or to explore these feelings and she would become overwhelmed at the power of them. It seemed that Lizzie had no internal mechanism to soothe herself (Winnicott, [1965]1987). We were curious at how frightening Lizzie might find this situation; the fragility of her future, her health, her behaviour in private and in public. But Lizzie could not share her psychological pain. In fact, we wondered if she even had the words to do so. We were curious about her early caregivers and wondered what they had felt and communicated to Lizzie when she was young and presented such overwhelming emotions. We thought about how her early relationship with her care givers may serve to organize her later attachment relationships (Bowlby, 1973). Lizzie was destructive in the group, breaking rules and testing boundaries. She would bring friends down from the landing to attend the group uninvited. She refused to come if she did not like other women in the room. She would refuse to engage at times and at other times would control the space so much it was difficult to even be there. We would often emerge from a group exhausted and confused about how difficult the group had felt. With Lizzie in the group, it was impossible to think. Her behaviour felt like an unconscious attack on the thinking within the group (Bion, 1962). We found ourselves feeling useless and incompetent and found we were aligning ourselves with her, unable to make connections or find meaning in the sessions.

Lizzie continued to destroy herself through her abusive, self-harming relationship with food, her long standing abuse of heroin and crack and her destructive capacities in the face of relationships. We wondered if her power to destroy; herself, others, her relationships, protected her from reliving the terrible feelings of loss, abandonment and rejection she had experienced as a child. Perhaps by becoming destructive she saved herself from being destroyed (Ferenczi, [1933]1980). Despite the difficulties, Lizzie attended the group every week. Paradoxically, while she dominated the group, it often felt that she was not really there. There was something inauthentic and unreal about her presence in the group. We wondered whether this counter-transferential feeling reflected something of how Lizzie felt about "being in the world". We wondered whether her assaults on her own body demonstrated a desperate attempt to "feel real". Perhaps as well as assaulting herself, her offences against the elderly were an attempt to exist and be seen in the eyes of her own parents. We wondered too how real the group felt to her. Lizzie spoke highly of it, and would often talk about how it "helped her survive" prison. But we were uncertain how much of the group she could make use of. Perhaps her behaviour in the group paralleled her behaviour with food; she could take in the nutrition, but could not hold it within her and would vomit it back. We wondered what she might be able to hold on to. She could accept treatment but seemed unable to absorb the care that was being offered to her by her medical team, spitting it out, unable to digest it (Bion, 1963). We wondered whether her own parents had been unable to think of her as a whole being. Her mother had left when Lizzie was eleven years old; approaching adolescence, becoming a woman. Perhaps Lizzie blamed her mother's rejection on her own growth into womanhood and was unconsciously forcing her body and mind to remain immature. Starving herself out of menstruation, using drugs to stop her intellectual development and presenting herself as a child.

Approaching an ending

As Holloway prepared to close, individual therapy was no longer available to the remaining prisoners. The group remained one of the few therapeutic spaces left where the women could think about their difficulties and the closure of the prison. However, the institution remained anxious about Lizzie's health, and an exception was made. It was decided that Lizzie would be offered four sessions of psychotherapy focusing specifically on her eating disorder. Because of this, Lizzie would be one of the last women to be moved. Her seemingly uncontainable anxieties continued to be projected into the institution, and now into me, her individual psychotherapist. It seemed as if therapeutic boundaries were impossible to maintain as the security of the prison walls began to diminish.

I now had a dual role as a co-facilitator of the group and Lizzie's individual psychotherapist. I thought I might be of some use.

However, I soon started to feel like one of her fashion accessories; another member of her entourage. Lizzie would often forget my name and refer to the "senior psychiatrist". I felt dismissed over and over again. I wondered whether Lizzie survived by denigrating attachment figures in an attempt to mitigate the pain of being abandoned by her mother and father. Perhaps her psychic survival necessitated dismissing the care she was offered. I also had in my mind Gianna Williams's work (Williams, 1997) in which she suggests that eating disorder patients experience being offered anything as an intrusive attack. Although Lizzie wanted help, it seemed that she wasn't able to take it in and instead punished me.

Working with Lizzie became yet another game of hide and seek. Like her index offence, where money was broken up and disappeared, it seemed that parts of Lizzie's own mind were fragmented and lost. I noticed too that in the counter-transference, I was losing my own mind in the session with her. I struggled to think clearly in the room with her, while outside I found myself pre-occupied with her. Rather like her bulimia, I felt empty and then immediately filled to the brim.

An extract from my process notes after a session with Lizzie:

> I am overwhelmed as I write this, she is so dangerous, to herself and others. I am so full of her. I am collecting up all the facts about her and it feels overwhelming. I became pre-occupied with her, thinking about her when I am not with her, when I am not working, at weekends, at home, but yet when I am with her I find it so hard to hold onto my own mind, myself.

Marilyn Lawrence suggests that whenever one meets a patient in the grip of an eating disorder,

> One knows that some kind of catastrophe has taken place. Without knowing how or why, it seems that psychically the patient has given up on the idea of relationships and crucially on any possibility of development. It is as though unconsciously some kind of decision has been made. All sense of relatedness to an object is lost.
> (Lawrence, 2001: 82,43)

In our work together, I tried to think with Lizzie about the part of her that, despite feeling protective, was protecting her only from making meaning of her life. I suggested to her that this internalized "protector" was actually lying to her, committing fraud by giving her deceitful messages. When I tried to bring any reality into the room Lizzie's mind would run away and it felt as if she was constantly dodging me.

One of the first writers to stress the importance control plays in the minds of these patients was American psychiatrist Hilde Bruch (1973). Bruch argued that the bulimic's need to control their objects was to the point of endangering their own lives. A binge may have represented in Lizzie her hatred and repudiation of the objects that, only minutes before, she had so greedily and cruelly devoured. Lizzie could not hold onto anything inside her, but I kept on hoping that she would be able to stay on the side of life, that she would become able to digest something and not spit it out.

Final thoughts

Lizzie experienced the sudden loss and rejection of her mother and father. It seemed that until she came to prison she had not experienced any consistent, reliable, loving relationships. She did not inhabit an environment where she was able to learn to safely contain and process her intense feelings and projections and negotiate the world and its difficulties. The closure of the prison may have confirmed her feeling that she could not be safely contained and this was felt too by her peers in the group and the professionals working with her. She did, however, exist for a short time in a group where she was thought about. It is our hope that she was able to internalize something of this experience in her journey towards understanding who she really is.

REFERENCES

Bateman, A., and Fonagy, P. (2004). *Psychotherapy for Borderline Personality Disorder: Mentalization-Based Treatment*. Oxford: Oxford University Press.

Bion, W. R. (1962). A theory of thinking. *International Journal of Psychoanalysis*, 43: 306–310.

Bion, W. R. (1963). *Elements of Psycho-analysis*. London: Heinemann.

Bowlby, J. (1973). *Attachment and Loss, Vol. 2: Separation: Anxiety and Anger*. London: Hogarth Press and Institute of Psychoanalysis.

Bruch, H. (1973). *Eating Disorders: Obesity, Anorexia Nervosa and the Person within*. New York: Basic Books.

Ferenczi, S. ([1933]1980). Confusion of tongues between adults and the child. In M. Balint (Ed.), *Final Contributions to the Problems and Methods of Psycho-analysis* (pp. 156–167). London: Karnac Books, 1980.

Lawrence, M. (2001). Loving them to death: the anorexic and her objects. *International Journal of Psychoanalysis*, 82(1): 43–55.

Welldon, E. (2011). *Playing with Dynamite: A Personal Approach to the Psychoanalytic Understanding of Perversions, Violence, and Criminality*. London: Karnac.

Williams, G. (1997). *Internal Landscapes and Foreign Bodies: Eating Disorders and Other Pathologies*. London: Karnac.

Winnicott, D. W. ([1960]1987). Ego distortion in terms of true and false self. In D. W. Winnicott (Ed.), *The Maturational Processes and the Facilitating Environment* (pp. 140–152). Madison, CT: International Universities Press.

Winnicott, D. W. ([1965]1987). The theory of the parent–infant relationship. In D. W. Winnicott (Ed.), *The Maturational Processes and the Facilitating Environment* (pp. 37–55). Madison, CT: International Universities Press, 1987.

PART IV

PRISON AND SOCIETY

CHAPTER TEN

Holloway and after

From loss to creativity

Sophie Benedict

An overview

Psychotherapy provides a relationship in which to explore the impact of loss and sees potential creativity in the process of working through the difficult feelings evoked by mourning; feelings of bereavement, abandonment, fury and violence are integral to therapeutic work.

The sudden announcement of HMP Holloway's close brought an immediate sense of loss to the psychological therapies service where I had worked for eight years. Following the announcement a period of confusion began for the staff as well as prisoners for whom Holloway had become a version of home. On the night of the announcement the prisoners all began singing from their barred windows; "We shall overcome. We shall not be moved."

Denying the reality of the news was understandable. Following this feeling of disbelief a period of mourning started with both staff and prisoners struggling to come to terms with the huge changes closing the prison would bring. The relationships between them had taken years in stressful circumstances to create. Facing staff and prisoners now, was the great uncertainty of relocation, loss of friends, even sadness at the loss of the building and gardens which had been home for many. For a time, staff and prisoners between them, shared many of the same feelings of anger and sadness. The doubt about what would happen next ushered in a new quality of tension in the air. This was easy to feel but hard to describe. The atmosphere at Holloway changed. Professional boundaries began to slip almost immediately, adding to the sense of instability behind the seemingly indestructible concrete walls. This was palpable in the demeanour and conversation between staff and was illustrated in a comment made to me by a prison officer in the immediate aftermath of the announcement. The very experienced woman grimaced as she shook her head in disbelief, sighed and said "You really couldn't make it up." This officer had worked in the female prison estate for over twenty years and her comment was a reaction to a number of incidents she had witnessed since the announcement. The rules were breaking down. Many of the women were acting out in extreme ways in response. Finally, the officer broke down in tears of exhaustion. I had never seen an officer cry before. Her colleagues attempted to console her but something felt like it was slipping away.

To me, HMP Holloway, with all the rules, rigid regime and restraints began to feel compromised on some level. The ambiguous future for the officers, healthcare staff and the prisoners seemed to lead to a kind of "laissez-faire" attitude by some of the professionals whose sense of purpose within the prison had been shaken. Seeing a male officer sitting with his feet casually on his desk brought this home to me. His physical statement of protest and contempt for the rules was visible to staff and prisoners alike. He seemed to be demonstrating his anger through his actions, as if there were no words or no one to listen to his fury. Acting out, a characteristic I had often recognised, erroneously, only in the prisoners, I now realised was unmistakable in the staff too.

My role in the prison

At the time the closure was announced, I was involved in the delivery of therapeutic interventions for women referred from around the prison for treatment. These women were discussed at the weekly referral meeting held on Wednesday mornings. Part of my job involved assessing the psychological capacity of the women with a view to offering them suitable treatment. I was employed in a dual role; by a charity called Women in Prison (WiP) and by the NHS trust contracted to deliver the healthcare provision in the prison. This included the psychological therapies team. Psychological therapies delivered a broad range of therapeutic interventions including group and individual psychotherapy, art therapy, dramatherapy, cognitive behavioural therapy (CBT) (Beck, 2011) and dialectical behaviour therapy (DBT) (Pederson, 2013).

Rumours of Holloway closing had circulated around the prison for many years but no one seemed to take them seriously anymore. However, when rumour gave way to reality, no one in the prison had been consulted or informed. There had been no consideration of the physical and psychological wellbeing of the vulnerable prisoners inherent in losing the only female prison based in London. The impact of the closure and the resulting loss was felt immediately. Considering the impact of the closure and the end of the therapeutic interventions for the women with whom we were working became our immediate focus. The loss of the therapeutic relationship, so hard to create and sustain, presented a risk of self-harm and acting out for the women. Ending therapy would result in a loss of perhaps the healthiest and most consistent relationship many had ever experienced; repeating and reawakening feelings of earlier losses. One women, Lisa, responded to the announcement by reflecting, "Not another loss. As soon as I get something good it is always taken away from me."

The reality of losing the only central London female prison became clearer as the "ship outs" of the women in the heavy, airless security vans started. Many were relocated, along with some of the Holloway prison staff, to HMP Bronzefield near Heathrow or HMP Downview in Sutton. Neither prison is in an area that is necessarily accessible or affordable to reach for friends and families of the women incarcerated there. Many women said that their families, so key to not returning to prison, would struggle to make such complicated journeys outside of central London. Women receive fewer visits if they are imprisoned far from their homes and this challenges their capacity to maintain relationships and family contact. Prisoners who are deprived in this way are up to six times more likely to re-offend within a year of release, while supporting family visits can reduce re-offending by 40 per cent (BBC, 2016). The mental health of both inmates and families suffer when a member goes to prison. Many thousands of children are separated from their mother through incarceration and children in this situation may show signs of anti-social behaviour and are more likely to offend themselves.

The prisoners we worked with in Holloway showed signs of trauma, sexual abuse and deprivation far greater than in the general population. As a group, the psychological therapies team provided a unique service to female offenders. Our collaborative work offered a way of "holding" our patients, with the anticipation that this holding would assist in developing or repairing the inner world of the patient. Holloway's closure repeated a pattern of abuse mirroring a cycle of neglect already familiar in their lives. This repetition was at the core of what we were trying to understand in our therapeutic work together. Now we found ourselves in an institution that was unconsciously replicating it.

Supervision

In my earliest days as a psychotherapist Karen Rowe supervised my training and encouraged me to consider a forensic setting as a way of developing my practice (Kahr, 2002). I was intrigued by her rigorous stance and eager to develop this approach in my work. Having been born and raised in Islington, HMP Holloway was a familiar institution for me, at least at a distance. Once inside the prison, Dr Paola Franciosi became my supervisor. She had many years of forensic experience and my practice is indebted to the training I gained under her thorough supervision. Dr Franciosi encouraged a transference based approach to psychotherapy. This offered a clear and helpful lens through which to consider these complex patients and the complex institution in which we worked. Supervision was personally demanding and there were several points where I nearly crumbled. My early supervision was at times as daunting as the face-to-face patient work. Learning to manage the challenges in supervision enabled me to face the therapeutic work. Nevertheless, the rigour and intensity provided a foundation that ultimately made the work more manageable. The supervision felt punitive at times, but I slowly began to realise this mirrored and reflected the environment. This gave me a robust framework from which to persevere, in addition to providing a space where I could take note of and understand better my own responses and potential for retaliation or boundary breaking.

Prisons have clear physical boundaries, demonstrated explicitly through the perimeter wall and razor wire. Psychotherapy in prisons entails reflecting on boundaries and acknowledging the boundaries that have been violated in the lives of the women. Therapy sets clear boundaries in order to give the patient an experience of containment. Having the session on the same day at the same time in the same place emphasised this. Consistent boundaries support the development of the relationship. Paradoxically, for many prisoners Holloway became a safe containing space that their lived experience had not provided for them. A high proportion of the prisoners had endured abusive and violent relationships. A lack of understanding about relationships therefore becomes an integral focus of the work. In addition to this however, it is important to add that I did not only see the forensic patient as a victim of their past. Through therapy as well as in psycho-education groups, CBT and other interventions, it is hoped the patient will come to see the role they have themselves played in their offending behaviour. With time and commitment, adhering to therapeutic boundaries and taking responsibility encourages the capacity to create more useful relationships in the future.

The women

My initial awareness of forensic patients began during my psychotherapy training at Mind. It was here that I had the opportunity to work with a former Holloway resident after her release. Beverley had been convicted of child cruelty and neglect. The abuse involved her own daughter who had fallen from a balcony when Beverley was intoxicated. Later at Holloway, I worked with several women whose offences included neglect or abuse of a minor. Over the years there has been an increase in women sentenced for abuse with a growing number of female child sex abusers coming into prison (Hislop, 2001). Working with women who have abused their children is a complex and difficult task for both the prisoner and the therapist. The importance of good supervision cannot be overstated as it is here the therapist has a space to manage the stress felt in hearing disturbing disclosures.

Beverley: the persistent offender

Prisoners can develop a love–hate relationship with the institution. Patients may consciously or unconsciously sabotage their right to freedom so that they can return to prison. Paradoxically, once they are incarcerated again they are angry about the restrictions. Beverley would regularly use her therapy to express her fury toward Holloway and all that the institution represented to her. Over the years she had been convicted of fraud, robbery and grievous bodily harm (GBH). Beverley had been in and out of prison the majority of her adult life and was thirty years old when we started weekly psychotherapy together.

Whenever Beverley returned to prison her mother would look after her six-year-old daughter. Furious in her sessions, Beverley complained about how much she wanted Holloway to be demolished. For her, the prison stood for something unbearable, perhaps a metaphor for her own life. In Beverly's mind the only way to keep from coming back to the prison was if the prison no longer physically existed. Her thinking was very concrete. An important part of therapy involves helping the patient think less rigidly. When Beverley was moved to a prison out of London she continued to rail again the existence of the prison, seemingly unable to explore or develop an understanding of why she kept repeating behaviours that guaranteed her return. As long as the patient places all the responsibility for their difficulties outside of themselves little change is possible. It takes a long time for such insight to develop and the frequent transfers and disruption of therapy in a prison stand in the way of this happening. When Holloway is eventually demolished, Beverley may find that her difficulties persist, even as the institution she has blamed no longer exists. Perhaps this will offer her an opportunity to think about her internal world as the external world around her changes.

Despite the difficulties inherent in prisoners becoming institutionalised, prison can provide the people incarcerated therein with an opportunity to work through the process of individuation. At its best, the prison stands in place of the parent providing a container for the prisoners feelings; setting clear boundaries which may have been absent at key developmental stages.

Carol: the mother on the mother and baby unit

Carol and I met while she was on the mother and baby unit with her son Callum. He was five months old at the beginning of our work together. Carol herself had been born while her own mother was in Holloway prison twenty years before. Like the children of many offenders, Carol had spent her life in and out of institutions in the care system. Carol's story clearly demonstrates the transgenerational pattern of repetitive offending. It is important that we try to learn from these examples and begin to understand on a wider scale why our structures deliver such poor outcomes. I conclude that we should use a more systemic approach not only to focus on the individual but to help us consider the cost to society (McCarthy and Simon, 2016). The stories of women like Carol seem to support the concept that when events cannot be remembered and worked through they are repeated with dire results.

A personal perspective

When I first began to work in Holloway I left my youngest child with a child minder. He was only a few months old. At times I felt torn and wondered if this separation from my own child would be worth the sacrifice. Despite my emotional upset and concern about my own family, there was something about working with these women that got under my skin. To me, the work offered rich rewards in terms of my own personal and professional development. Working with some of the most vulnerable women in the country showed me what a strain they are to themselves, to their families and to society. From a personal perspective I believe intrinsically in the work. I feel that supporting these women emotionally gives them the opportunity to think about their behaviour and to change. Most of the women held at Holloway had limited life chances to prevent them from going to prison. By offering psychological support I hoped to help them change the pattern of re-offending.

Ending

My final weeks at Holloway were sobering and sombre as therapeutic relationships came to an end. The final sessions with each patient were conducted with as much sensitivity as possible. Sadly, some women were transferred without warning, meaning there was no opportunity for a proper good bye. Losing their "home" was disturbing and prisoners on longer sentences, including life sentences, struggled with transfers. Some women reported increased thoughts of self-harm while others were acting impulsively to manage their anxiety. They all worried about how their families could keep visiting them once they were moved to less accessible prisons miles out of central London.

As well as giving more consideration to the impact of closure on the women, the psychological implications of the closure would have benefitted from more consideration of the staff experience. No one seemed to take this into account. The therapy work in the prison often entailed encouraging the women to think more about the possibility of understanding another person's perspective as different to and separate from their own. Indeed, the mentalisation-based treatment (MBT) model that has become fashionable in recent years concludes that individuals who are unable to think about the mind of another are likely to act out impulsively (Bateman and Fonagy, 2006). It seemed during the closure that the prison and the healthcare provider mirrored this incapacity to consider the impact of the closure on the staff. Nevertheless, in July 2016, the prison held a closing ceremony for staff in the gardens of the prison. The prison flag was lowered and presented to the longest serving officer in a moving ceremony which did, in some way, support the mourning process.

It is difficult to evidence the intricacies of our work in terms of the internal development in our patients but I have seen at first-hand how forensic psychotherapy encourages growth and understanding in our patients. This intensifies the pain we feel when we have to throw away our work even as we see it working. It will be difficult to count the cost of closing HMP Holloway, but inevitably there will be a price to pay. This might be seen both in terms of the loss for the individual losing her family contact, as relations are restricted due to the expense and difficulty in travel to these new locations; but also to society as a whole.

Looking forward: Holloway United Therapies

The joined up thinking we had strived for and that was embodied in the weekly referral meeting at HMP Holloway developed and nurtured professional and social contact. It had taken years to evolve the trust necessary for collaborative work and it was this teamwork that made the service so successful. Coming together for our regular clinical forums meant that, under the leadership of Dr Paola Franciosi, therapists and other interested colleagues had enjoyed a space to discuss and reflect on our differing specialities and the way we approached our work. These wonderful forums brought together various departments providing a platform to gain greater understanding of our differing roles as well as to develop closer relationships with other disciplines. Relationships are central to all creative work. The Saturday Forensic Forum, started in 2010, developed out of the Holloway clinical forums and now holds regular meetings for colleagues to continue and develop forensic psychotherapy based on the assertion that psychotherapy is of great benefit not only to the "worried well" but to the forensic patient.

Following the announcement of the closure of the prison, our team began to meet to discuss ways in which we could take the provision of therapy for offenders forward. After many hours of discussion we were resolute that something should be born from our work together. As a result Holloway United Therapies (HUT) was set up as a registered charity at the end of 2016 (see www.hollowayunitedtherapies.org.uk). HUT's principle is to deliver psychological therapies and interventions to women who have been involved in the criminal justice system. Holloway's historic site now sits in silence, awaiting its fate. The Reclaim Justice and Reclaim Holloway Networks were set up to fight for something more appropriate than luxury housing to be developed on the land. Along with these organisations, HUT is hopeful about being able to offer therapy on the site to reflect a lasting legacy.

Conclusion

HMP Holloway was originally designed to keep offenders at arm's length from society. Rebuilt as a women's prison from the 1970s, a greater emphasis on care for offenders with mental health problems entered the institution's thinking. However, most people who pass the building are untouched by the suffering that occurred behind the gates. Few think of the trauma contained within the high walls. It seems as if Britain chooses to remain unaware of the problems associated with incarcerating the highest number of people in Europe.

During my time at Holloway I worked with a woman who was on remand for a very serious charge. In therapy she described an event prior to her arrest. Driving in the car with her granddaughter, the child asked what the prison was for. My patient described responding adamantly that it was a place they would never encounter. To me, she expressed shame as she thought about her previous assumptions and how quick she had been to view offenders with disdain. As a society we hold on to the belief that keeping offenders locked up provides the best solution. While there are some disturbed and violent offenders for whom prison may provide the only way of keeping both the individual and society safe, as therapists we imagine that society could benefit by considering a different approach to those who end up in our penal system. In recent times we have seen an increasing number of voluntary sector organisations set up programmes for prisoners. Perhaps this reflects greater compassion and understanding towards offenders.

Following Holloway's closure several organisations that previously offered services to women in the criminal justice system either relocated or discontinued the services they provided. A number of us were made redundant in this process. This adds to the cumulative sense of loss. Staying focused on our goal to keep therapeutic work alive has felt like a fight at times, but has also provided a way of working through our own mourning.

This mourning was acerbated by the tragic and unexpected death of our colleague and supervisor Professor Gill McGauly in the month the prison closed. Gill supervised and supported us through the upheaval and uncertainty of the closure. A gracious and composed woman, she was a sustaining mentor to us in these difficult circumstances. Her sudden death was a personal loss that added to and overshadowed the other loses. Optimistic that HUT was a positive way to move forward, Gill encouraged us to keep our thinking alive. I will endeavour to keep her positive outlook in my mind as we continue moving forward with HUT.

At this time, no one can calculate the cost of the loss of Holloway in terms of services, jobs, professional relationships and the therapeutic work the women undertook. Perhaps if we aim for early interventions to support struggling, troubled individuals instead of financing punitive and disproportionate regimes, there will be less need for prisons. As a society we must respond in more creative ways to reduce offending. We must endeavour to support people to lead productive lives. In the meantime, as therapists, we are using the loss of Holloway to think creatively about different ways of reaching women whose lives have been indelibly affected by their imprisonment and contact with the criminal justice system.

REFERENCES

Bateman, A. and Fonagy, P. (2006). *Mentalization-Based Treatment for Borderline Personality Disorder*. Oxford: Oxford University Press.

BBC. (2016). Prison, My Parents and Me. BBC Children in Need documentary, broadcast 15 November.

Beck, J. S. (2011). *Cognitive Behavioural Therapy: Basics and Beyond*. New York: Guilford Press.

Hislop, J. (2001). *Female Sex Offenders: What Therapists, Law Enforcement and Child Protection Services Need to Know*. Ravensdale, WA: Issues Press.

Kahr, B. (2002). *Forensic Psychotherapy: Forensic Psychotherapy and Psychopathology*. London: Karnac.

McCarthy, I. and Simon, G. (2016). *Systemic Approach: Systemic Therapy as Transformative Practice*. UK: Everything is Connected Press.

Pederson, L. (2013). *Dialectic Behavioural Therapy Skills Training for Integrated Dual Disorder Treatment Settings*. Eau Claire, WI: PESI Publishing and Media.

CHAPTER ELEVEN

Trauma, art and the "borderspace"

Working with unconscious re-enactments

Jessica Collier

> *In all forms of art, part of you is in the trauma, and part of you is a step away from it.*
> (Angelou, 2002)

Introduction

On a winter afternoon my colleague and I were discussing our work in the shared psychological therapies office at HMP Holloway. One of the joys and benefits of working as part of this close and sympathetic group of clinicians was a sense that the opportunity for sensitive and confidential discussion, at times even much needed humour, was almost always available. Emotional support was freely given and perceived mistakes, slights or feelings of paranoia or frustration could be shared and thought about. On this occasion, while we were talking, there was a loud knock on the door. A well-respected senior officer, a woman of composure and integrity, told us we must go to a full staff meeting right away. Emotional and with a tear in her eye she said, "They're making an announcement. The prison is going to close."

In the prison chapel, at the exact moment the Chancellor of the Exchequer was making the announcement to the general public as part of his annual spending review, the governor told her staff the prison would be closing. Immediately people gasped and cried out. Then the room was filled with silence. There had been no warning, nobody had been consulted, no one had been informed. From the Victorian gothic splendour of the hugely opulent Houses of Parliament George Osborne explained that HMP Holloway, the only women's prison in London, would be shut and demolished as part of a wider closure of outmoded Victorian prison facilities. The duplicity of this statement was apparent immediately; the building of the current HMP Holloway was completed in the 1980s. This was not a Victorian jail infested with vermin and overcrowded, but a reasonably modern building offering a range of accommodation and often housing fewer than the number of women it had been designed for.

During an art psychotherapy session later on that day, one of my patients, a woman serving a long sentence who had spent much of her adult life incarcerated at Holloway, grappled with her feelings at the news of the closure. She was distraught at the impending loss and unable to process what was happening. She described the diversity of women she had known over the years and the different perspectives and ideas she had come to see. She stated she would be dead if it were not for Holloway, a sentiment I heard repeatedly in my seven years working there. As our conversation came to an end she described the prison as "like Mesopotamia ... it's a cultural haven. Where will we go?"

This was not a view shared by many. In the few media articles that appeared after the announcement, a single line was extensively quoted from the summary of, at that time, the most recently published inspection:

> Its size and poor design make it a very difficult establishment to run and in which to meet the complex needs of the often very vulnerable women held.

The lines following this were not quoted:

> ... most women, particularly the most vulnerable, were held safely and treated decently ... Women told us they valued being held close to their families and communities.
> (HM Chief Inspector of Prisons, 2013)

What were we to make of this? We were told our workplace and the home for many hundreds of vulnerable women must close because it was a Victorian prison, yet the building was completed in 1985. We were informed the prison was not fit for purpose, yet held vulnerable women safely and with decency.

There are many actual Victorian prisons in London that remain open, that weren't demolished as old Holloway Castle was in the 1970s, then rebuilt with the aspiration to offer psychological treatment to the women who would be accommodated there. The men's estate in London includes outdated Victorian buildings that continue to operate despite the over-crowded conditions and inherent violence. This raises the question as to why Holloway was really closed. Beyond the money procured from the cynical sale of ever increasingly valuable public land to private property developers, what did HMP Holloway symbolise and contain that was not wanted in our midst? Most importantly for this discussion, what was being re-enacted in the unplanned, rushed and ill-considered removal of this urban community; this cultural haven?

In this chapter I will think about what becomes of the space that is left behind, both physically and metaphorically, when something is removed. Once they have been isolated and are out of sight, perhaps we can forget about the women in our cities who have historically been neglected, abused and ignored. Concretely, we can think about the closure as a political move. In recent years, "austerity" policies mean many experienced prison officers have been laid off and replaced with cheaper staff. These new officers do not have the experience or understanding of the highly complex and multi-layered dynamics going on around them. While the government declares this a cost cutting exercise, we should remember the role prisoners have as an unconscious scapegoat for society and the collective function of institutional deprivation (Foucault, 1977). William Blake noted as long ago as the eighteenth century, in his *Songs of Innocence and Experience*, the significant role underprivileged members of society hold. This was a collection of poems commenting on the loss of innocence through fear and inhibition, social and political corruption, and by the manifold oppression of Church, State, and the ruling classes:

> Pity would be no more, if we did not make someone poor.
> And mercy no more would be, if all were as happy as we.
> (Blake, 1994)

I would also like to use the closure of HMP Holloway as a way to understand ideas around trauma, art and "borderspace". In particular, I would like to think about the unconscious re-enactments of damaging and distressing relational and familial dynamics. What was so striking about the sudden decision to close Holloway was how clearly it mirrored the thoughtlessness that permeates the prisoners histories and attachments; the unexplained severing of important ties; the alarming idea that one thing can simply be replaced by another and the apparent imperviousness to the scars that will be left; as if a place that has been bulldozed can be forgotten about like it never existed.

Additionally, the closure felt brutal, violent and senseless. A parallel perhaps of the terrible offenses some of these women had committed and the experience of their victims – of both the violence of the crime and the longevity of the consequences which may have to be endured over a lifetime.

Art making as a way to survive trauma

Hans Hack is a Belgian artist whose print series "Prison Typologies" takes the outlines of prisons throughout the world and makes works of art from them. He describes prisons as both invisible spaces and a sign for the relation between dignity and efficiency in a society. This contemporary idea reflects the views of Dostoevsky, himself a long term prisoner of the state, who famously suggested in the nineteenth century that "The degree of civilisation in a society can be judged by entering its prisons" (Dostoevsky, [1862] 1915).

The writing of prose and poetry and the making of art has been used extensively for memorialising lost people or lost spaces, although the questions and concepts these works pose often culminate in silencing or destruction. In the case of Rachel Whiteread's "House" – a cast of an entire Victorian house that was to be demolished by the council – the art work itself inspired a polarised and universally zealous reaction, much like HMP Holloway. It was itself demolished at the local council's behest, despite winning the Turner Prize. Similarly, the construction of Whiteread's Judenplatz Holocaust Memorial in Vienna, known as the Nameless Library, was protested against by local people on the basis, among other things, that it looked like a crate and was artistically worthless (Potterton and Leidig, 2000). Nevertheless, not all critics were hostile. Adrian Searle stated; "The building's emphatic muteness and silence is the appropriate response to the enormity of its subject. It will not disappear into forgetfulness or the every day. It is a place where memories happen" (Searle, 2000). The sculpture is now widely accepted as an important and meaningful memorial. "This monument shouldn't be beautiful", stated Simon Wiesenthal, who had commissioned the project; "it must hurt" (Connolly, 2000). This is art as symbol; as a holder of unspeakable thoughts and actions; a container of unimaginable loss.

But how do the often traumatised, emotionally neglected, uneducated women who have lived in Holloway and the staff who have worked, sometimes for decades, in the prison, recover from the trauma of losing *their* house, *their* container? Throughout history, even individuals who are not trained artists have used image making extensively to survive the trauma they have experienced. The feminist art historian Griselda Pollock writes that; "trauma explodes the typical distinctions between fiction and fact" (Pollock, 2010: 835). I believe art making allows traumatic experiences to be felt as fact, while mitigating the terror through the creative act. Art making gives a shape to something which hasn't yet been thought.

Images made by victims of the atrocities of the holocaust during the Second World War may at first glance look like illustrations of some fictional horror. But in fact, many were detailing the realities of the inhuman conditions and brutality the prisoners in concentration camps were subjected to. Halina Olomucki, a survivor who saved many of her pictures from Aushwitz-Birkenau wrote, "I had this incredible need to draw... to draw what was happening." She was told by her fellow prisoners; "if you live to leave this hell, make your drawings and tell the world about us. We want to remain among the living, at least on paper" (Novitch, Dawidowicz and Freudenheim, 1981). Through the making of images, men and women experiencing extreme trauma were able to acknowledge their own suffering while being conscious of the suffering of others. Through their art they were recognising the "unthought"; making the unconscious conscious. The creative act is used to mark both the present trauma and the possibility of a future in which the experience will be remembered and shared. Images contain meaning implicitly which may make not knowing and holding uncertainty more tolerable.

London artist Janetka Platun suggests that, "nothing is lost when it is creatively remembered" (Platun, 2015). This is true not just through the work of individuals but though the work of communities, cultural havens; through families and down generations. To paraphrase James Gilligan, human action and thinking is not just individual but also, unavoidably, familial, societal and institutional. Each of us is inextricably bound to others in relationship. All human action is relational (Gilligan, 1996).

Trauma re-enacted in prison

Bracha Ettinger, the Israeli artist, psychoanalyst and philosopher, talks about the gaps left in collective memory when trauma is not spoken about, when it is covered up and removed. She suggests generational trauma is amplified when gaps are left in history and holes are left unfilled in discussion. Where violence is committed, I would suggest this is at least partly due to the omission of acknowledgement or discussion of past trauma. Freud suggested that "wherever there is a symptom, there is also an amnesia, a gap in the memory" (Freud, 2014). I would suggest that survivors of trauma who openly share their experience, who express their feelings creatively, give themselves an opportunity to explore their own psychological and emotional responses in a way that those who stay silent cannot.

Of course, the women I worked with in Holloway may not have experienced the unimaginable level of social and political trauma survivors of concentration camps suffered. It could also be said that they were not "innocent" and had caused suffering to others. This must not be overlooked. Nevertheless, they had almost all experienced poverty, addiction, physical, sexual and psychological abuse or neglect and had been traumatised further by their own damaging, often violent, responses to this; and further still by the familial or societal response to their actions. Over the years working with women in Holloway, I found that often just being with someone, being close to another human being, was itself experienced as traumatic by patients at the beginning of therapy. Ettinger describes the attempt to connect with another's experience as, "wit(h)nessing" (Pollock, 2010). This is an aesthetic concept that brings together the notion of witnessing an individual's experience and feelings, while simultaneously being with them emotionally, of being present in their current telling of events. I have found this simple, yet deeply moving concept, invaluable when I have felt overwhelmed by the experiences my patients describe and when I feel unable to respond other than to "be with".

At Holloway it was not always possible for the women to feel heard, witnessed and worked with attentively. Their peers may often have had similar experiences, which could be shared between them. But both prisoners and staff often acted out their own problematic family dynamics, unconsciously re-enacting harmful, retaliatory ways of responding. Unsurprisingly, the women often chose to keep their feelings about their experiences to themselves, bearing the pain alone, hidden beneath layers of bravado. This choice to remain silent, the fear of speaking out, may unconsciously have mirrored the trauma that brought the women to prison in the first place. Using art within a therapeutic relationship – art psychotherapy – offers both the safety of what Bion described as "containment" (Bion, 1962) and the transformative process of creating something. Art making becomes both an event and an encounter. Griselda Pollock describes the act of making art as, "the passage to a future that accepts the burden of sharing the trauma while processing and transforming it" (Pollock, 2010: 830). I would suggest further that the space between the artist and the viewer, or the space on the blank piece of paper, becomes what Winnicott termed the "potential or transitional space". He suggested, "It is in the space between inner and outer world, which is also the space between people – the transitional space – that intimate relationships and creativity occur" (Winnicott, [1951]2012). Winnicott's idea of the potential space is eloquent and offers a beautiful metaphor for possible transformation though creativity. But I think Ettinger's concept of the "borderspace" adds nuance to the idea that creativity not only builds a foundation for relational intimacy but gives us the opportunity to understand ourselves as different but the same. She defines her idea thus:

> A borderspace is not a boundary, a limit, an edge, a division ... it is space shared between minimally differentiated partial subjects who, while they can never know each other, can, nonetheless, affect each other and share, each in different ways, a single event.
>
> (Pollock, 2010: 857)

In art psychotherapy, the room and the paper become both the potential space, where intimacy can be found and change can be made, and the "borderspace", where the act of creativity and "wit(h)nessing" happens. The art work becomes "...the threshold between the human pain of the past and the human compassion of the present" (Pollock, 2010: 860). It is when gaps are left unexplained, where trauma is unspeakable, where pain cannot be shared, that re-enactments happen. George Santayana very famously wrote that, "Those who cannot remember the past are condemned to repeat it" (Santayana, 2011). At Holloway this cycle of re-enacted trauma was evident in almost every woman I worked with.

Working with art and trauma

In the following clinical material I hope to demonstrate how these re-enactments can be observed, spoken about and responded to in art psychotherapy. I would like to thank this woman, whom I will call Kay, for giving me consent to use her images and to share some of the themes that came up in our work together.

Beginning

When we met, Kay was in her mid-twenties and had been sentenced for grievous bodily harm (GBH) with intent. Kay had been taking drugs and drinking heavily on the night of the offence. She had, for some time, been involved in a volatile relationship with a local man. She claimed that early on in the evening of the offence he had assaulted her. Over the preceding few months he had spread false rumours about Kay, mostly of a sexual nature, specifically that she had a sexually transmitted disease. She felt these rumours were damning and seemed unable to ignore them, apparently feeling shamed by the exposure of her sexual relationship with him. After the alleged assault, Kay had phoned a couple of male friends and they agreed to teach the man a lesson. Kay took her friends to his flat. He opened his front door, whereupon the men set upon him with hammers, while Kay offered directions and encouragement.

Kay showed no remorse for this attack, which left the victim with life-changing injuries. Indeed she reflected that they "should have finished him off" and had it not been for the stupidity of her co-defendants felt she could have "got away with it". James Gilligan suggests that "The purpose of violence is to diminish the intensity of shame and replace it as far as possible with its opposite, pride, thus preventing the individual from being overwhelmed by the feeling of shame" (Gilligan, 1996: 111). Kay's on-going apparent satisfaction with the harm she had caused her victim seemed in some way to protect her from the humiliation she had felt at the rumours he had spread.

Kay described the offence during our assessment meeting. We agreed to work together, and during the first session of art psychotherapy she quickly disclosed the sexual abuse she had endured from her father throughout her childhood. He was an authoritative figure, holding a senior position in the military, who was violent towards her mother and sexually assaulted Kay regularly from the age of six until she was twelve years old. These assaults would happen at night and Kay felt afraid of him. In the session Kay said she was not frightened of anything now except "daddy longlegs". She explained this was because "they come too close and won't leave me alone". I imagined at this very early stage that she was telling me about the residual feelings of fear she carried from childhood. I thought about the triumph she might have felt following her offence and how this triumphant feeling might have been converted from the trauma she had experienced as a child (De Zulueta, 1993). I wondered also if she might be telling me that she was frightened I would come too close and instructing me to stay at a distance. Kay's declaration that she was not frightened of anything might also have been an early indication of the depth of her dissociation from the trauma of her childhood.

Some weeks later Kay drew a punch-bag and two fighters. She told me she had never disclosed the abuse to any member of her family, fearing that her brother would kill her father, and that her mother would not be able to survive such news. Indeed Kay characterised her mother as a helpless "doormat" who was not strong enough even to visit her in prison. And so the gap where Kay's trauma existed seemed to have been there right from the beginning; in the silence and secrecy that surrounded her experience.

Kay told me about a dog she owned who was vicious and would bite old men if Kay did not act sufficiently like the "leader of the pack". It seemed to me that Kay was eager to show me how tough she was and her images accentuated this position. She drew a woman who you could not get near even if you were brave enough to try (Figure 11.1).

She is alone, loaded with weaponry and covered in vicious spikes and barbed wire. In addition to the defences Kay showed in this image, I also felt driven away from her verbally and emotionally. She would complain incessantly and unpleasantly about the inadequate care she considered she was receiving. It felt to me as if anyone who could show the capacity to care for Kay would not be allowed near. In the therapy this early pushing away and control extended even to the way she would make her drawings. Kay would hold a drawing board in front of her so I could never see what she was making unless she chose to show me herself.

Re-enacting trauma

As our work proceeded, Kay continued to complain that the prison could not take care of her. It seemed impossible to discuss or reflect

Figure 11.1

with her that this might mirror her own mother's inability to protect and look after her amid her father's control and abuse. Simultaneous to these discussions, Kay began to imply she was engaged in a "special" relationship with someone, although she denied this when asked directly. While she made an image of a wall, with shattered glass and blood all around it, Kay became angry and said that a peer had started rumours that she was having a sexual relationship with a member of staff. Kay said she wanted to "remove the eyes and mouth" of this peer. This seemed a remarkable parallel to the lead up to her offence. I thought of the feelings of shame she experienced at that time. I thought again of the violence and humiliation of her own violation as a child and her consequent violence later on. It seemed clear that if she was indeed in a relationship with a staff member then a damaging re-enactment was taking place and I knew I would have to find a way to attend to this.

Paola Franciosi suggests that "in the crime the patient reveals her internal world ... to try to make sense of how the internal world is played out in the outside world is the main therapeutic endeavour in the work with prisoners" (Franciosi, 2001). Attempting to understand this with the patient is vital. Nevertheless, as staff, and as therapists, we too unconsciously engage in the re-enactments played out by patients. Somehow my countertransference at this time was of feeling rather special to Kay and almost wilfully wishing to remain ignorant of the abusive interpersonal relationship she was engaging in. It transpired retrospectively that she had indeed started a sexual relationship with a staff member at this time. I realised later that I had overlooked this and was silent and oblivious, just as her mother had been. Thinking more profoundly about the countertransference I experienced, I realised too that this had been my own mother's modus operandi; overlooking the trauma both of her own life and that which emerged in front of her in an attempt to manage her loss and sorrow. Around this time Kay said to me "I wish I could take everything back I've said about my dad", as if unsaying the abuse would mean it had never happened.

In the next session, Kay declared, "My heart isn't broken anymore" and drew a couple, close together (Figure 11.2). I could no longer ignore what was so clearly before my eyes. I asked Kay what it might mean to be in a relationship with someone in authority, someone who might be taking advantage of her. Kay denied there was anything happening at all. I commented on how close to the edge of a cliff this couple are, the danger they are in. Kay replied, "I would not be that close to the edge if I was on my own", naming the implicit danger she placed herself in within relationships.

It has been proposed that individuals who are sexually abused as children are more likely to be sexually abused as adults, even that traumatised individuals seem to have an addiction to trauma (Van der Kolk, 1989). It seemed to me that as we had begun to discuss the trauma of her past sexual abuse Kay had begun to express her internal state through physical action, and was unconsciously compelled to repeat the traumatic relationship of her childhood.

Following this, Kay drew a group of elephants walking in line, holding on to one another but surrounded by lightning strikes. She said of the image, "If you touch an electric fence you do not touch it again". I suggested she might be telling me that the breaking of boundaries feels shocking. Kay thought this was ridiculous and told me I read too much into things. She then spoke again about needing to care for her mother and I began to feel that in the transference this might also be a need to look after me and our relationship; by denying

Figure 11.2

the abuse that was happening. My feeling of being protected by her continued as she drew a bucolic scene of a slow flowing river and weeping willows. As Kay drew she described how she and her mother would share their diazepam. This would tranquilise them and block out all their feelings of pain and difficulty.

Care and abuse

Kay then drew a vicious looking dog (Figure 11.3). When she turned her board around to show me the drawing I felt myself awakened from what had felt like my own tranquilised state of the previous weeks. Now more conscious of the reality of what was taking place, I tried to take up the corrupted and abusive relationship with her father and the apparent re-enactment of this with the staff member.

Kay, perhaps in her role as "leader of the pack", refused to speak about it and stated with determination "I do not see it as abuse".

Figure 11.3

Nevertheless, to me, while the dog looked angry and frightening it also appeared highly defensive. Michael Levy suggests that "defences lead to re-enactments and to the problems that the original defences sought to avoid" (Levy, 2000). Kay remained convinced that the healthcare staff, the cleaners and the prison officers were the people abusing their power. We were able to agree that the abuse of power upset her greatly. But Kay was unable to identify the actual abuser as abusive and rejected the idea of a pattern. She told me she felt it was me who was cruel and it became clear that Kay was not able to differentiate between cruelty and care. De Zulueta highlights how traumatic childhood abuse leaves the individual unable to differentiate between care and abuse, the two being linked inextricably (De Zulueta, 1993). It seemed that Kay's only hope of survival as a child might have been to identify with her abuser; to see the abuse as he might have seen it: "the most singularly devastating aspect of childhood abuse is the violent penetration and co-opting of mind that occurs when one is emotionally and physically dependant on another who violates and exploits" (Davies in Frankel, 2002: 104).

Eventually, the transgression of the staff member was responded to by the prison and he was dismissed. Having believed his promise to leave his wife and prepare for her release, Kay was furious that he had lied to her. She stated that she wanted to remove his balls. Simultaneously Kay was confused and felt guilty that he had been fired. She made an image of a flag with a kind of cage as its emblem and announced this was the banner of the "Nation of Kay", a place where only she would choose who could belong. I thought about this image as a momentary recognition of her profound isolation.

Kay's complaints against the prison and the staff increased and she told me I was making her feel like it was her fault when I tried to think about what had happened.

Kay made an image of a clown (Figure 11.4). She said she did not know if it was on the attack or the defence and she admitted she could not read anyone's motivations. Winnicott ([1960]1987) suggested that victims of abuse could become compliant, losing their sense of inner authority and self in their perpetual attempts to decipher other's motives; leaving them feeling false and detached. This constant scrutinising of intention "paradoxically results in both tremendous sensitivity and great blindness to others' motives" (Frankel, 2002: 114). Kay said I was not helping her and resolved to dismiss me as she felt I was manipulating her. She decided she wanted to go to the gym instead of therapy and I was reminded of the appalling physicality of sexual abuse. Bracha Ettinger reminds us of this when she describes trauma as, "saturated with corporeal and sensorial events" (Pollock, 2010). The timings of the gym session she selected clashed with the therapy. Kay told me it was I who was abusing her because I had declined to change our session time. She talked again about the abuse she suffered at the hands of her father, the violence she had encountered and how familiar it felt. Kay described the physical pain of being beaten and compared it with the physical and emotional pain she was currently experiencing. Kay told me, "my mum's right. It's better not to know what's going on", and she described feeling that if she did not agree to have sex with men they would reject her. She said, "it's like they don't care about my feelings."

I began to feel alone in the sessions as Kay drew images of barren islands. While she drew she spoke about her father leaving the family when she was twelve years old. Although for her the abuse stopped, the family had felt abandoned. Kay said before he left, her father had "handed her over" to one of his friends. Her mother's reaction to this was to put her on the contraceptive pill. Kay suggested, seriously, that

Figure 11.4

perhaps her father had abused her because she was irresistible. This felt like another explicit illustration of Kay's continued identification with the aggressor, as she tried in desperation to get onto the mind of her threatening father (Ferenczi, [1933]1980) I felt sad that she could

Figure 11.5

justify his behaviour in this way, but again Kay began to accuse me of not caring enough for her. The misidentification of her abuser as strong as ever, she told me she had had enough (Figure 11.5).

Ending

At this fragile moment in our work together, and without any consultation, Kay was put on a programme by the prison which clashed with our session. I had no authority to challenge this decision, again mirroring Kay's familial dynamics, and she missed weeks of therapy. In addition, Kay's newly appointed drug support worker told her she shouldn't do therapy if she didn't enjoy it; further cementing Kay's notion that it was I who was abusing her. There seemed to be numerous institutional obstacles to us continuing our work together and Kay appeared to utilise these. Eventually she told me I was "shit" and that I just made her feel guilty. As we thought about this Kay described to me how she liked to "fuck men until it feels too intimate"; then she

Figure 11.6

would get rid of them and replace them. Kay was doing well on the landing and had stopped self-harming. She told me she felt good now and could tolerate her moods better. She declared in our session, "You can't take all the credit."

In Kay's final session, with her own release imminent and the announcement of the closure of Holloway only weeks away, she presciently drew a scene from the novel *Watership Down* (Figure 11.6).

Richard Adams writes, "Like the pain of a bad wound, the effect of a deep shock takes some while to be felt" (Adams, 1972). In the eighteen months Kay and I worked together, we had attempted to navigate some of the shock she had supressed and endured since childhood. Prior to coming to prison this had been acted out in ways that mitigated her own feelings of shame and humiliation but which inevitably re-enacted the shocking trauma and violence she herself had been subjected to. Perhaps the gaps that had been left in her story had become an unconscious compulsion to repeat the brutal interpersonal relationships of her past. In Holloway these re-enactments continued, exacerbated by the impulsive, unconscious, complicity of staff and the implicit power dynamics and collusion within the therapeutic relationship. There was however, a material consequence for the individual who had explicitly abused his position. Some thought was given to how this had made Kay feel and how she might process what had happened. Importantly, Kay had also been offered an opportunity to "be with" another. In her art psychotherapy sessions, Kay had found a space where the abuse and trauma could be seen and, eventually, acknowledged.

In the novel, developers appropriate the rabbit's habitat to build luxury houses. The rabbits believe that "they destroyed the warren ... because we were in their way" (Adams, 1972). As she drew her final image, Kay described something good being taken from the rabbits. She spoke about the injustice of destroying the place where the rabbits had felt safe. Being forced to leave and move on for these rabbits, Kay said, would be dangerous, frightening and uncertain.

REFERENCES

Adams, R (1972) *Watership Down*. London: Puffin.
Angelou, M (2002) Maya Angelou prescribes arts for trauma survivors. *USA Today*, 18 February. Retrieved from https://usatoday30.usatoday.com/news/health/spotlight/2002/02/18-angelou-spotlight.htm.
Bion, WR (1962) *Learning from Experience*. London: Heinemann.
Blake, W (ed.) (1994) The human abstract. In W Blake, *Songs of Innocence and Experience*. Princeton, NJ: Princeton University Press.
Connolly, K (2000) Closed books and stilled lives. *The Guardian*, 25 October. www.theguardian.com/world/2000/oct/26/kateconnolly
De Zulueta, F (1993) *From Pain to Violence: The Traumatic Roots of Destructiveness*. Ann Arbor, MI: Whurr, University of Michigan.
Dostoevsky, F (1915) *The House of the Dead* (translated by C Garnett). New York: Macmillan.
Ferenczi, S ([1933]1980) Confusion of tongues between adults and child. In M Balint (ed.), *Final Contributions to the Problems and Methods of Psycho-Analysis*. London: Karnac Books.
Foucault, M (1977) *Discipline and Punish: The Birth of the Prison*. London: Penguin Books.
Franciosi, P (2001) The struggle to work with locked up pain. In J Williams Saunders (ed.), *Life within Hidden Worlds: Psychotherapy in Prions*. London: Karnac Books.

Frankel, J (2002) Exploring Ferenczi's concept of identification with the aggressor: Its role in trauma, everyday life and the therapeutic relationship. *Psychoanalytic Dialogues* 12, 101–139.

Freud, S (2014) *Five Lectures on Psychoanalysis*. London: Read Books.

Gilligan, J (1996) *Violence; Reflections on Our Deadliest Epidemic*. London: Jessica Kingsley.

HM Chief Inspector of Prisons (2013) Report on an unannounced inspection of HMP Holloway. London: Author.

Levy, M (2000) A conceptualization of the repetition compulsion. *Psychiatry: Interpersonal and Biological Processes*, 63(1), 45–53.

Novitch, M, Dawidowicz, L and Freudenheim, T (1981) *Spiritual Resistance. Art from Concentration Camps, 1940–1945*. New York: Union of American Hebrew Congregations.

Platun, J (2015) Cuming: A natural selection. www.peckhamplatform.com/whats-on/exhibitions/cuming-a-natural-selection

Pollock, G (2010) Aesthetic Wit(h)nessing in the era of trauma. *EurAmerica: A Journal of European and American Studies*, 40(4), 829–886.

Potterton, L and Leidig, M (2000) Holocaust tribute by British artist divides Vienna. The Telegraphy, 26 October. www.telegraph.co.uk/news/worldnews/europe/austria/1371869/Holocaust-tribute-by-British-artist-divides-Vienna.html

Santayana, G (2011) *The Life of Reason: Introduction to Reason and Common Sense*. Cambridge, MA: MIT Press.

Searle, A (2000) *Austere, Silent and Nameless – Whiteread's Concrete Tribute to Victims of Nazism*. The Guardian, 25 October.

Van der Kolk, B (1989) The compulsion to repeat trauma: Re-enactment, re-victimization and masochism. *Psychiatric Clinics of North America*, 12(2), 389–411.

Winnicott, DW ([1960]1987). Ego distortion in terms of true and false self. In DW Winnicott (ed.), *The Maturational Processes and the Facilitating Environment* (pp. 140–152). Madison, CT: International Universities Press, 1987.

Winnicott, DW ([1951]2012) *Playing and Reality*. New York: Routledge.

Afterword

Jessica Collier and Pamela Windham Stewart

In the summer of 2016 the last women left HMP Holloway and were moved out of London to prisons across the country.

Two years later, the women who were moved on from the prison but remain incarcerated continue to think about and remember their time there. On more than one occasion women who were resident have eagerly declared that HMP Holloway is going to be re-opened; they have asserted confidently that this will happen because the female estate is bursting at the seams; they have admitted, quietly, that they miss it.

For many years nostalgia was seen by psychologists as detrimental, not as a response to feelings of loneliness or isolation, but as the very reason for those feelings. More recently, however, nostalgia has come to be seen as a kind of defence mechanism; a way of building resilience through difficult experiences and surviving times of vulnerability or deprivation. Anecdotal evidence suggests thinking about better times helps us to overcome present adversity, even when these memories are idealised. This phenomenon was notable with survivors of concentration camps, who endured starvation by sharing nostalgic reminiscences about memorable meals and favourite recipes.

As noted throughout this book, for some women, incarceration at HMP Holloway was the first opportunity they had been given to think about themselves; to feel listened to or noticed. If there is some nostalgia felt about HMP Holloway, it seems important to recognise that despite its many shortcomings and the reckless speed with which it was closed, it offered for those women, the possibility to make meaning of lives which had previously been imbued with shame and worthlessness.

Don DeLillo writes that, "Nostalgia is a product of dissatisfaction and rage. It's a settling of grievances between the present and the past" (1985). If this is the case, the psychotherapeutic work that was offered at HMP Holloway can be remembered – nostalgically perhaps – as an attempt to make sense of stories, lives and personal tragedies, not as moralistic lessons to be learned, but as insight into how and why women commit crime. The testimony and experience documented in *The End of the Sentence*, the on-going dissatisfaction and rage, obliges us to inspire a more creative, curious and compassionate debate about female offending.

REFERENCE

DeLillo, D. (1985). *White Noise*. New York: Viking.

INDEX

abandonment 2, 14–15, 95, 139, 145, 147, 153, 177
abuse 3, 13, 62, 86, 102, 103, 130, 137, 138, 166, 169, 177; see also child abuse; sexual abuse; patterns of 54, 156; of power 176, 181; of substances see alcohol addiction drug addiction
Accredited Offender Behaviour programme 16, 18
"acting out," 41–2
Adams, Richard, *Watership Down* 180–1
addiction 47, 49, 74, 86, 88, 169, 174; see also alcohol addiction; drug addiction
Adlam, J. 14, 49
Adshead, G. 14
Aiyegbusi, A. 15
alcohol addiction 74, 125, 128, 129
Amiga, Sabina 5
Angelou, Maya 164
Anti-Social Behavioural Order (ASBO) 139
Armstrong, D. 14
art therapy 5, 39, 41–2, 60, 91, 101–20, 155, 166–81
assault 53, 74, 126, 171; see also self-harm; sexual violence
Assessment, Care in Custody and Teamwork (ACCT) 116, 118
asylum seekers see foreign nationals
Atkinson, Zoe 5
attachments 2, 13, 14, 66, 130, 145, 147, 167

Auschwitz-Birkenau 168
austerity, violence of 9–21
autism 95
Awang, H. 112
Aylesbury prison (Buckinghamshire) 9

babies see Born Inside project Mother and Baby Unit
Barnardos 28
Barrett, J. 14
Bartellas, K. 28
Bartlett, A. 130
Bateman, A. 13–14, 138, 160
BBC 155
Beard, Barbara 60
Beck, J. S. 155
Bell, D. 36, 37
Belsky, J. 14
Benedict, Sophie 5
Bennett, R. 9
Bentham, Jeremy 132
Bick, Ester 23
Bion, W.R. 103, 107, 109, 110, 115, 145, 146, 170
Birth Companions 11
Blake, William, *Songs of Innocence and Experience* 166
border experiences 72–3, 74
borderline personality disorder 47, 82
"borderspace," 165–6, 170
Born Inside project 4, 23–38
Bowlby, J. 128, 145
British Medical Journal 59

Bronzefield Prison (Surrey) 33–4, 38, 155
Brown, C. 116
Bruch, Hilde 147

Camarena Altmairano, J. 115
Campbell, Donald 64
Canham, Hamish 109–10
Carlen, Pat 10
Case, Caroline 103, 107, 113
charitable and voluntary organisations 10–12, 13–15, 33, 61, 67, 68, 90, 91, 161–2; *see also* Holloway United Therapies (HUT); Women in Prison (WiP)
Charles Dickens, *Oliver Twist* 28–9
child abuse 14, 64, 65–6, 67, 91, 130, 157, 175–6; *see also* child sexual abuse
child loss, therapy for 91
children of prisoners, impact on 3, 28, 35; *see also* Born Inside project
child sexual abuse 50, 51, 157, 173, 174, 175, 176, 177–8; disclosure of 171–2; women as abusers 157
Clarke, Ken 127
Clarke, Peter, Chief Inspector of Prisons 129
Clean Break 11
Clear, T. 36
Clerici, M. 28
clinical forums 35–6, 63, 160–1
Clinical Outcome in Routine Evaluation (CORE) 2
closure of Holloway 1–2, 3, 5, 10, 12, 13, 19–21, 32, 33, 38, 110, 141, 142, 146, 148, 160–1, 164–5, 166; announcement (2015) 9–10, 33, 110–11; loss, sense of 5, 14–15, 21, 32, 110–12, 118, 134, 153–6, 159–60, 162, 165; reflections on 14, 69, 95–7, 167
cognitive behavioural therapy (CBT) 142, 155, 157
collective memory 169
Collier, Jess 38
collusion 17, 106, 131, 181
Committee of 100 11

Committee of Enquiry into Medical Care in Holloway (1919) 9
Community Mental Health Team (CMHT) 82
'Concrete Mother,' 14, 76, 78
Connolly, K. 168
Converse Prison News 129
Corston Report (2007) 19, 21, 33, 102
costs of imprisonment 28
countertransference 46, 106, 174
Criminal Justice Act 2003, 124
criminal justice system 2, 11, 12, 17, 67, 68–9, 102, 123, 127, 134, 162; *see also* Imprisonment for Public Protection (IPP)

Dawidowicz, I. 168
deaths in prison 19; *see also* suicide
Delshadian, S. 102, 110
deprivation *see* neglect and deprivation
destructive unconscious behaviours 115–16
De Zulueta, F. 172, 176
dialectical behaviour therapy (DBT) 155
disrupted attachments 2, 14
Doctor, Ronald 20
Dokter, D. 52
domestic violence 91
Dostoevsky, F. 167
Douglas, N. 28
Downing, Lorna 4, 41, 43, 44, 54
Downview Prison (Sutton) 38, 155
dramatherapy 4, 41, 155; counter-transference, working with 46–7; pregnant therapist and 41–55; safe space, creating 45–6
drug addiction 5, 28, 29, 37, 73, 88, 103, 109, 125, 126, 128, 129, 171; crack 14, 139, 145; heroin 48, 139, 141, 143, 145
drugs offences 28, 29, 37–8, 88, 103
Dudley, J. 114

eating disorders 5, 140, 141, 142, 145, 146, 147–8
Edwards, D. 109, 113, 119
"emotional wellbeing," 132
Emunah, Renée 41–2, 51
Ettinger, Bracha 169, 170, 177
evidence-based therapy 20–1
experience-based therapy 20

'false self,' 143
Fazel, S. 28
Fearon, R.M.P. 14
Ferenczi, S. 145, 178
Fitzpatrick, R. 28
Fonagy, P. 13–14, 130, 138
foreign nationals 28, 33; deportation 105, 106, 109; marginalisation 102; Onyx art therapy group 5, 101–20
forensic forums *see* clinical forums
forensic psychotherapy 29, 33–4, 36, 59–71, 74, 90, 92, 127, 157, 160–1; females, lack of services for 64, 70; index offence, consideration of 62, 130, 137; principles of 138; risks in 79; therapist responsibility 76–7
Foster, H. 28
Foucault, M. 29, 102, 132, 166
Franciosi, Dr. Paola 4, 34, 59–71, 156, 160, 173–4
Frankel, J. 177
Freudenheim, T. 168
Freud, S. 104, 169
funding 12–13, 20, 80, 88, 107, 108

gender bias, in sentencing 131
Gergely, G. 130
Gilligan, James 168, 171
Gladwell, M. 35
Gordon, John 137
Gove, Michael 33
Grandison, R. 44
Greenham Common protesters 11
Griffins, The 11
group therapy 5, 17–18, 50, 63, 91, 142–8, 155; *see also* Born Inside project; dramatherapy; Onyx art therapy group

Grout, Lorraine 4, 43, 44, 54
Guardian, The 33, 127

Hack, Hans, "Prison Typologies," 167
Hannah-Moffat, K. 16
Havsteen-Franklin, D. 115
Hayes, A. 28
health care staff 85, 87, 89–90, 96–7, 154
health care unit 14, 41, 43, 44, 45, 47, 49, 89
health of prisoners 16, 30, 31, 53, 86, 87–9, 140–1, 145, 146; *see also* alcohol addiction; drug addiction; eating disorders; mental health
Heaven, Olga 33
Hibiscus 11, 33
Hislop, J. 157
HM Chief Inspector of Prisons 129, 165; *see also* Ramsbotham, David
Holloway Castle 165
Holloway, P. 52
Holloway United Therapies (HUT) 11, 160–1, 162
Holocaust memorial 167–8
homelessness 2, 20, 52, 86
Home Office 69
House of Commons 95
House of Lords 21

immigrants *see* foreign nationals
Imprisonment for Public Protection (IPP) 5, 124, 126; therapeutic work with IPP prisoner 123–35
Independent Monitoring Board 89
Independent, The 28
index offence: *see also* non-violent offences; violent offences; consideration of, in forensic psychotherapy 62, 130, 137
infant observation 23–4; *see also* Born Inside project
Inquest 10
institutional dynamics 4–5, 59–71, 72–84

IPP *see* Imprisonment for Public Protection
ISIS 11
Isserow, J. 120

Jani, R. 112
Jennings, S. 42, 51
Judenplatz Holocaust Memorial (Vienna) 167–8
Jurist, E.L. 130

Kahr, B. 156
Kennedy, A. L. 6
key performance indicators (KPIs) 95, 96
Klimt, Gustav *The Kiss* 25
Kurdish Freedom Party 11

Lawrence, Marilyn 147
Leidig, M. 167
Lemma, A. 131
Lennon, Siobhan 5
Levy, Michael 176
Lewis, C. S. 1
Lomas, Martin 3
loss 3, 15, 49, 74, 78, 109, 118, 143, 144, 148, 174; *see also* abandonment; art as container of 168; of a child 91; feelings of, on closure of Holloway *see* closure of Holloway

McCarthy, I. 159
McCoy, Catherine 5
MacDonald, M. 28
McGauley, G. 34, 130, 162
Maclennan, Frances 5
Mansfield, Maureen 4
mental health 2, 3, 25, 28, 50, 60, 74, 88, 94, 103, 132, 155, 161; arts activities and therapies 41–2; *see also* art therapy; dramatherapy; funding cuts, effect of 88
mental health team 3, 12, 16, 18, 34, 77, 81, 82, 85, 94, 96
mentalisation 130, 138
mentalisation-based treatment (MBT) 160

Mind 157
Ministry for Justice 116, 124
mirroring 50–1, 115
mother and baby groups *see* Born Inside project
Mother and Baby Unit (MBU) 25–6, 27, 30, 32–3, 34, 38, 69, 158
mothers and mothering 13–14, 52
Motz, Anna 14, 42, 46–7, 50, 52
multi-agency public protection arrangements (MAPPA) 133–4
Murray, J. 28

National Institute for Health and Care Excellence (NICE) 87
National Lady Visitor Association 9
National Offender Management Service 116
neglect and deprivation 13, 14, 60, 77–8, 83, 89, 102, 103, 135, 155–6, 166; childhood 129, 137, 157; *see also* child abuse; emotional 60, 62, 65, 66, 112, 143, 168, 169; patterns of 54, 156; physical 62, 66, 88, 112, 169
Newgate Prison 9
NHS 5, 11, 44, 63, 65, 67, 68, 85, 89, 96, 154
non-violent offences 2, 88, 105, 116, 138, 158; *see also* drugs offences
Novitch, M. 168

observation *see* Born Inside project
Olomucki, Halina 168
Onyx art therapy group 5, 101–2, 102–20
Osborne, George 165

Pandora's Box 109
panopticon 86, 132
parole board 16, 18, 124, 125, 127, 133, 134
Pederson, L. 155
personality disorders 47, 82, 95
Platun, Janetka 168
Plugge, E. 28
political prisoners 3, 11
politics of prison 4, 12, 166
Pollock, Griselda 168, 169, 170, 177

Portman Clinic 62, 64, 70
post-partum psychosis 50
Potterton, L. 167
poverty 3, 86, 112, 143, 169
pregnant inmates 23, 25–6, 34, 35, 42, 63
pregnant therapist 41; changes in transference 43, 46–7; conflicting responsibilities 45, 46; dramatherapy and 4, 41–54
Prison Announcement (2015) *see* closure of Holloway
prisoner referral model 94
prison intelligence unit 132
prison population 2, 27–8, 86
prison reform 9, 11
Prison Reform Trust 2, 28, 36, 101, 126, 127, 133
prison staff 3, 29, 44, 50, 59, 66, 69, 77, 86–7, 92, 130, 140, 142; *see also* probation service; and austerity policies 166; and closure of Holloway 153–4, 155, 159–60; and health care staff 85, 89; sexual relationship with inmate 173–4, 176, 177; and therapeutic staff 81, 87
prison system 11, 14, 28, 33, 70, 110, 126
probation service 16, 18, 34, 61, 90, 94, 125, 131, 134
professional dynamics 4–5, 72, 79–84, 91–3
prostitution 14, 113
psychoanalytic team 81, 82
psychological therapies service 1–2, 11, 18, 36, 44, 51, 54, 59, 140–1; *see also* forensic psychotherapy; attitudes to 63–5; closure of Holloway and 1–2, 95–7, 153–62, 164; development of 5; Franciosi/Rowe conversation 4, 59–71; management of 85–6, 90–7; measuring success 67–8; motivations of therapist 13, 36–7; specific issues in Holloway 65–7
psychology department (Holloway) 60

Radical Alternatives to Prison (RAP) 10
Ramsbotham, David, Chief Inspector of Prisons 25, 26, 42
Reclaim Holloway 10, 13, 161
Reclaim Justice 161
Reed, S. 24
re-enactments 52, 110, 133–4, 139, 170, 176; trauma 169–70, 172–5, 180; unconscious 5, 131, 164, 166–7, 169, 174
Reeves, Chrissy 5
'reflective functioning,' 13–14
reflective practice groups 34, 38, 61, 62
release from prison 14, 32, 83, 105, 116, 126, 129, 177; *see also* parole board; re-offending; post-release support 4, 18, 67, 68, 70, 133, 157
re-offending 14, 33, 35, 155, 159
Robins, L. 35
Rothwell, K. 41, 44, 110
Rowe, Karen 4, 59–71, 156
Russell, Mary, duchess of Bedford 9

Sainsbury Centre for Mental Health 127, 132
Salzberger-Wittenberg, I. 15
Santayana, George 170
Saturday Forensic Forum 35, 160–1
Saunders, Jessica Williams 42
Scanlon, C. 14, 49
Searle, Adrian 167
Second World War 168
Seebohm, H. 52
self-harm 43, 47, 74, 77, 103, 116, 118, 133, 140, 145, 146, 155, 159, 180; managing 87; rituals of 48
self-inflicted deaths 19; *see also* suicide
sentencing 2, 16, 17; *see also* Imprisonment for Public Protection (IPP)
separation unit 14
Sexton, A. 55
sexual abuse 60, 138, 155–6, 169, 174; *see also* child sexual abuse

sexual relationships, with prison staff 173–4, 176, 177
sexual violence 91, 113, 171–2
sex working *see* prostitution
Simon, G. 159
Sinek, S. 95
Spinoza, Benedict de 36
Stewart, Pamela Windham 4
Stokoe, P. 15
Strout, E. 29
Styal Prison (Cheshire) 19, 33
substance abuse 94; *see also* alcohol addiction; drug addiction
suffragettes 3, 11
suicide 19, 43, 45, 46, 47, 75, 116; attempted 28; ideation 43, 74, 77, 103–4, 116
supervision 4, 24, 34, 36, 64, 71, 75, 92, 93, 106, 115, 128, 156–7; groups 60, 62, 94, 127–8; joint 114

Target, M. 130
Taylor, B. 36
Tchaikovsky, Chris 10, 12
Teasdale, C. 106
transference 62, 75, 131, 147, 156, 174–5; *see also* countertransference; changes in 43, 46–7
transfers of prisoners 16, 18, 97, 109, 116, 142, 159; disruption to therapy 27, 44, 64, 68, 158
trauma 2, 3, 5, 13, 15, 74, 88, 102, 155, 161–2; *see also* loss; addiction to 174; art therapy 103–4, 110, 116, 164, 166–81; disconnection from 104; dramatherapy 45–55; early 112, 129, 172; re-enactment of, in prison 169–70, 172–5, 180; re-traumatisation 95
Treasures Foundation 11
Trestman, R. 28
Turner Prize 167

Van der Kolk, B. 174
Victorian prisons, closure of 9–10
violent offences 18, 35, 37, 50–1, 64, 73, 74, 91, 158, 161, 171; *see also* assault; sexual violence
voluntary organisations *see* charitable and voluntary organisations

Welldon, Dr. Estela 32, 42, 64, 137
Whiteread, Rachel 167–8
Wiesenthal, Simon 168
Williams, Gianna 147
Wilson, Kimberley 4–5
Winnicott, D.W. 42, 76, 103, 110, 143, 145, 170, 177
Women in Prison (WiP) 9, 10–18, 19, 21, 154; funding 12–13; services provided by 91
Women in Secure Hospitals (now Women at WISH) 11
women's organisations 12–13; *see also* charitable and voluntary organisations
Wong, L.P. 112

Yakeley, J. 14